Al-'Arabiyya

Journal of the American Association of Teachers of Arabic

العربية

مجلة رابطة أساتذة اللغة العربية

Volume 51 | 2018

Al-ʿArabiyya: Journal of the American Association of Teachers of Arabic
Volume 51 (2018)

Editorial Office
Email all editorial correspondence to aataeditor@aataweb.org

Professor Mohammad T. Alhawary, Editor
University of Michigan
Department of Middle East Studies
202 S. Thayer Street, Suite 4111
Ann Arbor, MI 48104-1608
http://aataweb.org/alarabiyya

Publisher (purchase and copyright)
Georgetown University Press
3520 Prospect Street NW, Suite 140
Washington, DC 20007
http://press.georgetown.edu

Al-ʿArabiyya (ISBN 978-1-62616-651-6; ISSN#: 0889-8731) is published annually by the American Association of Teachers of Arabic.

Institutional and Literary Library Subscriptions: A single issue of *Al-ʿArabiyya*, which is published annually, or a one-year subscription may be purchased by institutions and libraries for US $60. Place orders at 800-537-5487 or online at http://press.georgetown.edu. Beginning with volume 47, *Al-ʿArabiyya* is also available as an e-journal through Project MUSE.

AATA Membership: A subscription to *Al-ʿArabiyya*, which is published annually, is included in a membership to the American Association of Teachers of Arabic (AATA). The annual cost of membership is US $50 for individuals, US $15 for students, and US $200 for institutions. AATA welcomes members who live and work throughout the world; AATA does not have a residency or citizenship requirement for members. For more information about AATA membership, to join AATA online, or to download an AATA membership application, please visit the AATA website at http://aataweb.org/signup.

Back Issues: Printed back issues through Volume 43 are available through the AATA website at http://aataweb.org/purchase_publications and can be ordered for US $35 each for institutions/agencies and US $20 each for individuals. Printed back issues from Volume 44-45 (2011–2012) forward are available from Georgetown University Press for US $60 each. Digital backlist volumes are available online through JSTOR and MUSE.

Advertising: AATA is pleased to accept a limited number of advertisements, which appear after all editorial content in *Al-ʿArabiyya*. For information about advertising your institution, organization, publications, or other products or services that relate directly to the needs and interests of AATA members and subscribers, please contact the Editor at aataeditor@aataweb.org.

Membership subscriptions: If your subscription copy of *Al-ʿArabiyya* has not yet reached you, please contact AATA at 3416 Primm Lane, Birmingham, AL 35216 USA. Phone 205-822-6800, fax 205-823-2760, info@aataweb.org.

Contents

Editor's Note

The present volume of *Al-ʿArabiyya* includes five articles, four of which are quite timely. They contribute to ongoing debates in their respective subfields: Arabic foreign language pedagogy, Arabic sociolinguistics, Arabic historical linguistics and dialectology, translation and language change/development, and modern Arabic literature and criticism.

Through his review article, John Eisele problematizes advocating exclusive efficacy of one approach to teaching Arabic as a foreign language. He argues that the choice of implementing one approach, be it Munther Younes's integrated approach or any other one, is not a simple one, as it must necessarily take into account other crucial factors, most prominent among which are linguistic reality, linguistic dissonance, and linguistic choice.

Similarly, through his study findings, Thomas Leddy-Cecere questions the prevalent paradigm of conflating variation in style with diglossic register. He calls for further replication studies and for the identification of diglossic shifting as a phenomenon involving switching between two distinct sets of phonetic norms rather than style shifting within the same norm.

The article by Peter Glanville deals with the grammaticalization of the construction consisting of the particle *ši* preceding a noun phrase. In particular, Glanville proposes a reanalysis where, starting from the lexical source, *šay'* "thing," the construction developed diachronically through the sequence: Partitive > Quantifier > Determiner > Approximator.

Maria Swanson examines Leo Tolstoy's influence on Mikhail Nuʿayma (or Naimy, as he used to spell his last name) and the moral concerns that both shared. She does so by focusing on two novels written by the two authors (Tolstoy's *The Kreutzer Sonata* and Naimy's *Memoirs of a Vagrant Soul* or *The Pitted Face*) and offering a literary and psychoanalysis of the two protagonists in both works.

Shehdeh Fareh discusses the impact of translation on the Arabic language. He provides a brief account with specific examples illustrating the role of translation (through its different forms) in changing or developing the language lexically, semantically, metaphorically, and syntactically.

The book review section contains six reviews. It includes Uri Horesh's review of Youssef A. Haddad and Eric Potsdam's *Perspectives on Arabic Linguistics XXVIII: Papers from the Annual Symposium on Arabic Linguistics*; Paul A. Sundberg's review of Andreas Hallberg's *Case Endings in Spoken Standard Arabic: Statistics, Norms, and Diversity in Unscripted Formal Speech*; Yahya Kharrat's review of Mahdi Alosh and Allen Clark's *Ahlan wa Sahlan: Functional Modern Standard Arabic for Beginners*, 2nd ed.; Janelle Moser's review of Mahdi Alosh and Allen Clark's *Ahlan wa Sahlan: Functional Modern Standard Arabic for Intermediate Learners*, 2nd ed.; Maher Bahloul's review of Nasser M. Isleem and Hajer Al Madhi's *Arabic Language in the Emirati Films: Linguistic and Cultural Window on Emirati Films*; and Sawad Hussain's review of Jonas M. Elbousty and Muhammad Ali Aziz's *Advanced Arabic Literary Reader: For Students of Modern Standard Arabic*.

I am pleased to present the articles and book reviews contained in this volume of *Al-ʿArabiyya*. I hope readers will find them beneficial in many respects and that they will stimulate continued discussions and inspire more publications and further research.

—Mohammad T. Alhawary

Acknowledgments

I would like to express my sincere gratitude to the following people for serving as referees for volume 51 of *Al-'Arabiyya*. Their generous contributions of time and expertise contributed to the quality of this volume.

Ahmed Idrissi Alami
Abdulkafi Albirini
Ahmad Al-Jallad
Mahdi Alosh
Ahmad Alqassas
Enam Al-Wer
Maher Bahloul
Brahim Chakrani
John Eisele
Joseph Farag
Nathaniel Greenberg
Nancy Hall
Sam Hellmuth
Zeinab Ibrahim
Ghada Khattab
Margaret Litvin
Christopher Lucas
Mohammad Mohammad
Mustafa Mughazy
Dilworth Parkinson
Abdulkareem Said Ramadan
Karin Ryding
Spencer Scoville
Usama Soltan
Driss Soulaimani
Keith Walters

One Path or Multiple Paths

MUNTHER YOUNES ON THE INTEGRATED APPROACH TO ARABIC INSTRUCTION

■

John Eisele, College of William & Mary

A review of Munther Younes's monograph *The Integrated Approach to Teaching Variation* uncovers several issues that need to be addressed in a more comprehensive manner. These include linguistic variation (sometimes termed diglossia), the integrated approach (teaching dialect or dialects simultaneously with teaching Standard Arabic or *fuṣḥā*), interdialectal intelligibility, linguistic reality, linguistic dissonance, and linguistic choice. In examining these issues, a claim is made that there are multiple ways of dealing with them depending on the interests, goals, and abilities of the instructor and program. In addition, the article discusses issues of proficiency evaluation in Arabic in light of these matters.

Key words: integrated approach, linguistic reality, linguistic variation, linguistic choice, linguistic dissonance, interdialectal intelligibility, proficiency and variation, evaluation procedures

Introduction

Since the beginning of the proficiency movement in Arabic language pedagogy in the 1980s, Munther Younes, professor of Arabic at Cornell University, has been an indefatigable proponent of teaching colloquial initially and eventually simultaneously with Modern Standard Arabic (MSA) in the course of teaching Arabic during the first several years of instruction. For many years he was a voice in the wilderness, but in recent years he has been joined by one of the most influential groups of Arab pedagogues, namely, the authors of the series *Al-Kitāb fī Taʿallum al-ʿArabiyya,* published by Georgetown University Press. Younes has recently published a short monograph that outlines his approach and gives evidence to support his approach based on his experiences in teaching Arabic. In reviewing this monograph, I would like to give it the attention it deserves but present as well an alternative view that also does not give short shrift to the issues of teaching colloquial Arabic. The monograph is relatively short (fifty-eight pages), and one might wonder why it would need such a lengthy review. However, the issues that Younes deals with are some of the most pressing issues facing the field of Arabic language pedagogy, and the ideas presented in his monograph have recently gained great currency in the field and require some comment. It should be noted also that this article is meant as a preliminary response to recent efforts in the field that have tried to handle the phenomenon of diglossia, and is not the last word on the topic. Finally, this article aims to stimulate discussion in the field of a dispassionate and unbiased nature.

Overview

Younes begins his monograph by noting that the teaching of Arabic as a foreign language has been plagued by the issue of diglossia, a term introduced in Ferguson (1959), who attempted to provide a framework to describe linguistic variation in the Arab world.[1] Younes's solution to this problem is to propose the notion of an "integrated" language program in which the two varieties of Arabic (*fuṣḥā* and *ʕāmmiyya*) are introduced simultaneously, which reflects, according to Younes, how the language is actually used by native speakers. Integration, he claims, is the most logical, effective, and economical way to prepare students of Arabic as a foreign language to deal successfully with the diglossic situation, and he sets out to prove this. The book is divided into five chapters: Chapter 1 summarizes academic writings on diglossia, chapter 2 addresses the needs of students of Arabic in a university setting, and chapter 3 reviews the unsatisfactory approaches used so far. In chapter 4 he describes his integrated approach, noting its advantages over other practices, and in chapter 5 he reviews and dismisses possible objections to his approaches.

Chapter 1 starts with an extremely good and thorough review of the literature on the notion of diglossia, starting with Ferguson (1959). The articles that followed were not so much challenges to Ferguson, as Younes states, but rather attempts to refine the notions set forth in the original article, based on the notion of there being levels between *ʕāmmiyya* and *fuṣḥā*. A feature of these articles that is not clearly brought out by Younes is that they were all (with the exception of Bishai [1966], who dealt with recorded speeches delivered from written texts) dealing with spoken Arabic, not written, and from the earliest (Blanc 1960) it was recognized that the levels being adumbrated were for the most part colloquial speech at their base, with various admixtures of *fuṣḥā* accounting for the differentiation into levels.

The recognition that the middle forms being described in almost all the articles on diglossia represent spoken modalities of Arabic, being at base essentially colloquial forms of the language modified by more or fewer elements of *fuṣḥā*, is an important insight. It is one, however, that is at one point lost in Younes's analysis when he makes the claim that written MSA is essentially the written counterpart of Educated Spoken Arabic (ESA): "The variety of Arabic designated by this name [MSA] is in fact Modern Standard *Written* Arabic. It is the written counterpart of what I have called in Chapter 4 LESA and other ESA varieties" (16).

The easy identification of ESA with written Arabic is incorrect, in my view. The justification for this view comes from Dilworth Parkinson (1991), who described different evaluations of forms of written versus spoken Arabic in Egypt. In short, the expectations regarding speech are that it is colloquial, while the expectations regarding written texts are that they are in *fuṣḥā*. If elements of *fuṣḥā* are encountered in speech, then that speech is evaluated as being more like *fuṣḥā* even if the amount of *fuṣḥā* elements is negligible. On the other hand, if elements of colloquial are encountered in a written text, then that text is evaluated as being colloquial, even if the amount of colloquial is in fact quite small. In other words, the expectations and evaluations of spoken Arabic and written Arabic are mirror images of each other, and it would be a mistake, in my opinion, to see one as being the simple counterpart of the other.

The second topic dealt with in chapter 1 is interdialectal intelligibility, a topic, as Younes notes, that is rarely studied. It is, however, one that forms an important part of his methodology. As he states, "If dialects are mutually intelligible, then the learner who masters one variety will be able to communicate with speakers of other mutually intelligible varieties" (13). Also, because of mass education, satellite TV, movies, and the like, "the concept of a plain uneducated vernacular has practically disappeared" (14). While I think that Younes is extending his generalization of the phenomenon far too much, it is at base a valid observation. Note, however, the phrase "other mutually intelligible varieties," which seems to imply that there are varieties that are not mutually intelligible.

Following this discussion, Younes discusses the notion of a standard language, especially regarding what is termed *Standard Arabic*. He gives a quick overview of the history of Arabic teaching in the United States, where the term *Modern Standard Arabic* was coined in the title of the dominant textbook of the time, the "Orange Books," *Elementary Modern Standard Arabic*. I think his point regarding the misleading nature of the term *standard* in *Modern Standard Arabic* is valid, but he does not offer an alternative term or way of thinking about what "Modern *Fuṣḥā*" is: if it is not a standard in the normal, European sense of the word, then what is it? This points to a general shortcoming in Younes's approach as contained in this volume: rather than being a dispassionate account of the phenomenon of variation in Arabic and how to deal with it pedagogically, it seems to be more of a polemical account, attempting to provide justification for his methodology of integrated instruction in Arabic as contained in his textbooks.

The limitations of this approach become most apparent in his further discussion of the notion of mutual intelligibility, whether between the various Arabic dialects or between the dialects and *fuṣḥā*. The first step in this argument is that *fuṣḥā* and *ʕāmmiyya* are essentially the same, based on the previously stated notion that ESA is essentially colloquial for the most part: "In spite of the grammatical and lexical differences between *Fuṣḥā* on the one hand and any of the *ʕĀmmiyya* varieties on the other, most of the grammar and lexicon are shared by the two" (18). The next step is to reiterate the observation noted earlier, that ESA is essentially a colloquial base to which are added elements from *fuṣḥā*, and that this constitutes the medium of pan-Arab communication. Thus, rather than *fuṣḥā* being the element that unifies the Arabs in their linguistic communication, it is the mutually intelligible varieties of *ʕāmmiyya* that perform that function: "One could make the case then that the colloquial base, shared by the various Arabic *ʕĀmmiyyas*, enriched by *Fuṣḥā* words and expressions, and not *Fuṣḥā* exclusively, unifies the Arabs linguistically at the practical, conversational level" (19).

Before moving on to a discussion of this argument, it should be noted that it could be used equally well to support the teaching of *fuṣḥā* first, followed by teaching of a dialect or dialects, given the great similarity between all the varieties. I will return to this point later. The main issue I have with this argument is that neither of its claims is proven or exemplified. If one were to compare the varieties of Arabic at different linguistic levels (which I do in the appendix to this article), such similarities would be evident, but such a comparison would also serve to exemplify the many great differences between these varieties. In a later section Younes downplays these evident differences, but they cannot be so lightly disregarded. In taking issue with Younes on this point, I do not intend to argue against the efficacy of his approach but to argue that there is space enough to argue for other approaches, even using some of Younes's own arguments, depending on which aspects of Arabic one sees as being important in constructing a program and a methodology for teaching Arabic. I will return to this point in my commentary.

Chapter 2 deals with changing student goals in the study of Arabic, pointing to the increased interest among students of Arabic in pursuing the goal of speaking proficiency above other goals, and chapter 3 details the ways in which traditional Arabic programs fail to meet these objectives. In chapter 3, I believe Younes was reliving arguments from the past forty years or so with traditional Arabic (and Arab) pedagogues and bringing in student observations from a period in which the linguistic reality of Arabic language variation was hidden from students or downplayed; this before the days of the internet and Google, when students could easily get this kind of information on their own with a few clicks of the mouse. I think that most students of Arabic today are well aware of Arabic language variation and of the necessity of learning a dialect as well as *fuṣḥā*, and of the benefits, if not necessity, of study abroad in achieving these goals. In a similar vein, Younes tries to paint with one brush both the ideologically charged traditionalists who reject any mention of dialects in an Arabic classroom and those who choose, for other reasons, to focus on *fuṣḥā* initially, especially in programs outside of the Arab world. I doubt that very many of the latter would believe that a dialect could be "picked up" off an Arab street like chewing gum sticking to one's soles. A final comment on these observations is the repetition of the experiences of students who, upon entering a taxicab in Cairo, are laughed at for using *fuṣḥā*. In response, I would like to mention my own experiences of using Egyptian Arabic in Morocco, which engendered smiles and laughter among the local inhabitants because I sounded like someone from the movies (Egyptian ones, that is), a reaction I also found with other non-Egyptian Arabs unfamiliar with foreigners who could speak Arabic with some proficiency. By recounting these experiences, I do not mean to suggest that one should not learn Egyptian dialect but rather that encounters with native speakers who are not familiar with foreigner speech in Arabic may give rise to some embarrassing situations, not all of them tied to whether one's program is integrated.

Chapter 4 describes the author's experience with his own integrated language program at Cornell University, where he has been quite successful in training students using his method; in this chapter we learn that the colloquial he is integrating is actually a form of ESA from the Levant, specifically the author's own Palestinian dialect hybrid. Chapter 5 deals with possible objections to his program. We will discuss some of the issues that are brought up in this chapter in the following discussion.

The arguments that are brought forth by Munther Younes in this book for using an integrated approach to teach Arabic variation are not entirely convincing, at least to this reviewer. Many of these arguments contain valid observations and do bring to the fore an important point that is necessary to consider seriously—namely, how to deal pedagogically with the widespread and actively exploited variation in Arabic languages or dialects. Rather than phrasing the problem in terms of "Which one first, colloquial or *fuṣḥā?*" where there is an expectation that there will be one correct answer depending on one's ideological bent, I believe it is more useful and beneficial to consider the problem from multiple vantage points and to leave open the possibility that there are multiple paths that are pedagogically sound and depend on the abilities, outlook, and proclivities of programs and instructors. It is important, however, that whatever approach is followed, programs must include instruction in an Arabic dialect or dialects or must provide an overview of dialect variation. The question is not dialect or no dialect but finding the most efficacious way of instructing students of Arabic in the ways of Arabic linguistic variation, whatever the context may be.

Teaching Arabic Variation: Linguistic Reality, Linguistic Dissonance, and Linguistic Choice

In his short monograph, Munther Younes confronts some of the issues that Arabic language pedagogy today—more so than at any time in the past—has had to confront. His book, however, while containing many valid observations and insights, is geared toward one goal—namely, proving the efficacy and validity of his own integrative methodology. In this section I briefly outline the issue in larger terms, which may encompass multiple paths toward achieving proficiency in Arabic language variation. We will consider these issues from three aspects: the linguistic reality (namely, the wide variation in Arabic types), linguistic dissonance, and linguistic choice.

Linguistic Reality

The reality of the Arabic language situation as it confronts learners and pedagogues is that there are many different varieties of Arabic, each with its own distinctive cultural and communicative significance and each requiring acquisition of competence in it as well as competence in mixing them. Past practice of ignoring this variety until several years into learning MSA is recognized as insufficient, and neither does teaching only MSA serve learners adequately; consequently, there has been a paradigm shift recently away from *whether* to teach colloquial toward *how* to teach it.

Younes, in trying to find support for his methodology, deemphasizes this variation, choosing instead to focus on the common elements shared by the varieties of Arabic, including *fuṣḥā* and the dialects. And common elements there are, as shown in tables A1 through A3 in the appendix, which compare features of phonology and inflectional and derivational morphology across the varieties of Arabic. On the phonological level (table A1), it is important first of all to note the great deal of similarities in the reflexes of early Arabic sounds in *fuṣḥā* and the dialects and to note those points at which they differ, which indicate important isoglosses in the dialect continuum and are sometimes the clearest markers of dialect distinction in the language. The shared features of inflectional morphology in table A2 are remarkable, showing one major isogloss between Maghrebi and Mashreqi dialects—namely, the first-person singular and plural in the non-past-tense verb (the imperfect). The same level of similitude is also present in table A3, which details the derivation morphologies among the varieties of Arabic. In addition, as Younes notes, ESA (his version of a "dialect") contains a great many words borrowed from *fuṣḥā*, which are shared by educated speakers from all dialect areas.

In addition to these sites of similitude in the phonology, morphology, and educated lexicon, the other tables detail sites of dissimilitude at the syntactic level (including negation, interrogatives, demonstratives, and verbal tense prefixes) as well as at the common lexical level (tables A4 through A8).

Until recently, Arabic language pedagogues have not felt the need to deal with the multiplicity of this linguistic reality and instead have relied on the traditional approach to teaching Arabic—namely, through teaching MSA, even while using proficiency-oriented methodologies that emphasize four skills (speaking, listening, reading, writing). However, recent trends have been forcing Arabic language professionals to confront and deal with this linguistic reality head on, and in doing so many have expressed concern about two issues: that teaching a dialect along with MSA will create confusion (linguistic dissonance) and that choosing which dialect to teach early on (linguistic choice) imposes something of a Hobson's choice on an instructor, a program, and the field as a whole.

Linguistic Dissonance

Linguistic dissonance is defined here as the confusion created in adult learners by having to learn two different forms of a second or nonnative language simultaneously. It may be viewed from the perspective of both the learner and the instructor. From the learner's point of view, learners expect to deal with a consistent and logical set of structures and behaviors, and dissonance often occurs when a learner is given a choice between two or more linguistic structures that express the same or similar things but in structurally distinct fashions: for example, expressing "I want to go" as either *'urīdu 'an 'aδhab* (MSA) or *'āyiz 'arūḥ* (Egyptian) or *biġīt nimši* (Moroccan), and so on. Confronting this variation early in the learning process could lead to a linguistic dissonance on the learner's part, resulting in stalling the learner's progress in acquiring the language. A similar dissonance may also be brought about from the instructor's point of view: teachers have a desire to maximize clarity by focusing on specific aspects of the target language in their presentation. Dealing with multiple structures from multiple target language varieties will tend to decrease this clarity and focus and increase the instructor's dissonance, which could further exacerbate learners' dissonance. Initial attempts to reduce this dissonance generally take the form of teaching only one form at a time, and this is the logic of many in the field of Arabic language pedagogy who maintain that teaching MSA is the best way to proceed, at least for the first few years of language instruction. (Of course, behind that logic some may also find the fourteen-century tradition of Arabic language ideology, which only sees value in the classical Arabic language and its linguistic tradition of grammar and grammarians). Dealing with possible linguistic dissonance in this way, however, means not dealing with *linguistic reality* for several semesters or years, if ever, and this is becoming more and more unacceptable in the field. In dealing with Arabic linguistic reality, then, it may not be possible to avoid linguistic dissonance completely, but any program set up to do so should take the issue of possible learner dissonance into account in devising its program of instruction.

Linguistic Choice

In confronting the linguistic reality of Arabic variation, having first determined that linguistic dissonance is something that must be considered in dealing with it, one is then confronted with a question that may not have an easy answer—namely, the choice of which variety or varieties to teach. The predominant choice up to now has been to teach MSA, whether in a traditional translation-and-grammar approach (which has become increasingly rare in the United States) or using a modified proficiency-based approach that simplifies MSA a bit, usually taking out the case system and modifying it into a kind of "Educated Spoken Arabic." The main drawback of this approach, as noted previously, is that it avoids the linguistic reality of Arabic in which the "conversational" skills (speaking and listening) are carried out in a form of colloquial, while the reading and writing skills are carried on through the medium of MSA. In turning away from this traditional approach, one is then confronted by the multiplicity of Arabic dialects from which one must choose a medium of instruction for the proficiency-oriented classroom. If a program or a textbook chooses one, then it in a sense has excluded others in the linguistic reality; it is also paying primary attention to only one aspect of the proficiency program—that involving the conversational skills (speaking and listening). In a sense, it devalues the writing and reading skills (carried out in MSA) and deals with only a "slice" of the linguistic reality—that of the region served by the dialect (usually Egypt or Syria).

The point behind this discussion is to show that the choice is not an easy one, nor should it be, given the complexity of the situation. Pretending that it is, by choosing one dialect as the basis for the instructional program, is addressing Arabic linguistic reality only in a limited fashion. It is, moreover, an approach that is forced on the field by the constraints of the proficiency methodology itself, which values conversational skills over printed medium skills, as is reflected in the more highly developed evaluation metrics for conversational skills over written skills. In reviewing the various approaches that follow, it is important to keep in mind these choices and the reasons that are given by those who make the choices in order to evaluate to what degree they deal with the linguistic reality of Arabic variation and avoid linguistic dissonance in doing so. It should be noted that there is no one "correct" way to address these questions but simply various possibilities that instructors or programs may use to achieve the goals that they set for themselves and for their students.

Dealing with Variation and Dissonance: Possible Arabic Language Curricula

There are basically three ways of teaching Arabic linguistic reality or variation. First, teach MSA, then deal with a dialect or dialects; second, teach a dialect first, then deal with MSA; third, teach both simultaneously. In considering each of these, we will pay attention to the issue of how each confronts linguistic reality, how each deals with possible linguistic dissonance, and how each makes choices about the variety to teach.

MSA First and Dialect Later

The most common approach today is to start teaching Arabic solely focused on MSA for several semesters before having students study a dialect. This approach puts high value on avoiding linguistic dissonance on the part of both learner and instructor but also puts off dealing with linguistic reality to an unforeseeable future. Within this approach, one may discern widely differentiated programs ranging from the unadulterated translation-and-grammar approach, which dominated Arabic language studies up until the 1980s, to approaches that clearly apply proficiency methodologies to teaching MSA, including implementing it through all four skills. It is the latter type that has come under fire by some for ignoring linguistic reality and having students carry on conversations in

MSA that are more appropriately done in a dialect. Proponents of this approach usually counter with the "avoiding linguistic dissonance" argument—that it "avoids inundating the learner with multiple registers from early on, avoids the insoluble issue of dialect choice (that would have to be made on behalf of most learners), and avoids programmatic confusion as students change teachers within the same institutions or without" (Alhawary 2013). Also mentioned in this regard is the avoidance of fossilization of early learners' errors, given the high level of dissonance, as well as an attention to other aspects of "linguistic reality," which are given short shrift in dialect-first approaches—namely, the goal of developing an "educated native speaker competence" in the written medium as well as formal and semiformal spoken contexts of Arabic.

Dialect First, Then Switch to MSA

This approach has been attracting more and more adherents in recent years. Generally, the approach starts entirely with a specific dialect (usually Egyptian) for a semester and in the following semester focuses primarily on MSA, using colloquial for classroom talk. Examples of programs following this type of curriculum are the University of Amsterdam (using Manfred Woidich's *kullu tamām!* textbook), Western Michigan University (using Mustafa Mughazy's *Dardasha*), and Brigham Young University. This approach places a high value on confronting linguistic reality by starting out with a dialect for simple conversational skills, and it deals with linguistic dissonance by separating out the varieties for at least a semester. The question of linguistic choice for this approach has so far always devolved on Egyptian (Cairene) Arabic, with the claim that Egyptian Arabic functions as a kind of "lingua franca" in the Arab world.

A variation on this approach is found in Munther Younes's "integrated approach," which starts with a Levantine Educated Spoken Arabic (LESA) and then gradually integrates more and more MSA into the lessons. This approach is similar to the previous one in placing high value on dealing with linguistic reality, but it uses a different approach for dealing with linguistic dissonance—namely, a gradual infusion of MSA exemplars instead of a complete switch, with the claim that this is a better reflection of linguistic reality than other approaches. Linguistic choice for this approach has so far devolved on Levantine Arabic (or LESA), which is the native dialect of the author, Younes.

Simultaneous MSA + Dialect

A more recent addition to the possible curricula for teaching Arabic variation has appeared in the third and newest edition of the most widely used series of Arabic language textbooks, *Al-Kitāb fī Taʿallum al-ʿArabiyya* (Brustad, al-Batal, and Al-Tonsi 2011), which reflects practice developed over the past few years at the Arabic program of the University of Texas. This approach may be best described as a full-frontal assault on Arabic linguistic reality, presenting simultaneously vocabulary and basic grammar for three different varieties—MSA, Egyptian, and Levantine Arabic. In doing so, however, it sacrifices any attempt to avoid linguistic dissonance and seems instead to promote it. In terms of linguistic choice, it is again far out in the lead, offering three possible varieties for the instructor and learner, not just the usual one.

A variation on this method (bearing great similarity to Younes's approach) was offered by the late Waheed Samy, who suggested the "hybridization" of MSA with colloquial features—that is, using an existing MSA curriculum as the basis onto which are integrated elements of a colloquial. This approach represents a middle ground between valuing linguistic reality and avoiding linguistic dissonance: the introduction of colloquial elements gives learners a more realistic representation of Arabic in use, but the gradual introduction of these elements into an MSA curriculum is meant to minimize dissonance. Linguistic choice may be limited to one particular dialect, depending on the instructor, as well as an accompanying set of colloquial features. The result of this choice is a kind of Arabic with linguistic features falling on the continuum between MSA and colloquial—as illustrated by panel discussions on pan-Arab TV. This is a proposal that has not yet been implemented.

MSA Base with "Elements of Dialects"

This approach differs from the previous in that elements from more than one dialect are introduced into the MSA base. The goal of this approach is to equip learners with knowledge about core "rules" that give them a superficial yet beneficial understanding of common underlying themes in the way a colloquial form is spoken and to make correspondences between standard and spoken varieties of Arabic. Examples of this approach are found in the textbook *Kullo Tamam, Tout va bien: Arabe niveau,* volume 2, by Klibi-Séassau and colleagues (2007). In this text, alongside the MSA texts and dialogues, elements of four dialects (Moroccan, Tunisian, Egyptian, and Lebanese) are intertwined into the course with explanations of the differences in pronunciation, grammatical rules, morphology, and syntax.

Another possible approach to handling this aspect of Arabic instruction could be to focus on MSA in the core textbook, with each chapter including a "linguistic culture" segment that exemplifies a variety of colloquial elements from a different dialect. In addition, as part of this approach, each major dialect area could also be provided with a separate textbook. This approach gives equal weight both to addressing linguistic reality and to avoiding linguistic dissonance: introducing basic elements from more than one dialect gives a more realistic picture of Arabic linguistic variation, but giving each variety a separate textbook allows learners and instructors to focus on one variety at a time, thereby decreasing possible learner dissonance. Linguistic choice

Table 1. Summary of Approaches

	linguistic reality	linguistic dissonance	linguistic choice
1. MSA first	avoids	avoids	MSA
2. Dialect first, switch to MSA	engages	avoids	one dialect
3. Simultaneous MSA/dialect	confronts	increases	MSA + 2 dialects
4. MSA + elements of dialects	engages	lessens	more offerings

in this approach is left up to the instructor and program, allowing learners a wider range of possible dialects to learn and laying the foundation for the development of multidialectal comprehension at advanced and superior levels.

Summary

In comparing these approaches to each other (see table 1), it is clear that the choice of one over the other depends on which of the three aspects of the Arabic linguistic situation an instructor thinks is the most important. If avoiding linguistic dissonance is what you value most, and dealing with linguistic reality is not that important, then the MSA-first-and-only curriculum seems acceptable. If, however, you want an approach that deals in some measure with the reality of linguistic variation in Arabic, then one of the other three approaches may be more of what you are looking for. If avoiding dissonance is high on your list, then the third approach (simultaneous MSA + 2 dialects) may not be what you are looking for since it seems to invite dissonance rather than avoid it. The second and fourth approaches, however, offer some ways of avoiding or lessening dissonance even as they deal with variation, the main difference being in the kinds of choices available: the second approach restricts the type of dialect offered to one, while the fourth approach offers multiple dialects tailored to the personnel and interests of a program. In reality, the kinds of materials being developed for the textbooks proposed in the fourth approach could be used in a program that looks like one, two, or three, with the additional information on dialect variation contained in the core MSA textbook.

Arabic Linguistic Reality, Dissonance, and Choice: Implications for Evaluation Procedures

As the preceding discussion shows, the application of proficiency-based methodologies has had a great impact on the way that we teach Arabic, and the field is currently in a state of flux because of it. The same may be said of the impact that proficiency-based evaluation procedures have had on how we evaluate Arabic second-language (L2) learners. The first ACTFL guidelines for Arabic speaking proficiency were developed in the late 1980s under the guidance of Roger Allen (Abboud et al. 1989), and one sees in them an avoidance of dealing with variation in Arabic, at least at the lower levels of the evaluation scale. For example, a learner could be evaluated as anywhere from Novice High to Advanced Low without giving any indication that he or she has any proficiency in a dialect. In discussions that occurred around the latest revisions (ACTFL 2012), it was proposed that more attention be accorded to proficiency in a dialect at the earliest levels, to the extent that speaking exclusively in MSA at this level would result in a lower evaluative rating. Although these proposed revisions were not included in the final guidelines, these kinds of problems are due in large part to the nature of the scale itself, which was developed to evaluate learners of French, German, or Spanish. When this kind of scale is applied to the evaluation of learners of a language like Arabic, with a high degree of linguistic variation and a clear split in the ways the four skills divide up among the potential varieties, it is clear that something does not fit.

Before turning to a consideration of how the skills fall out in the context of Arabic, it is important to make some qualifications in how the skills are best understood. The breakdown of skills into four types (speaking, listening, reading, and writing) is not adequate to the needs of assessing learners of any language, let alone one as variable as Arabic. I believe that it is best to make a further differentiation among each of the skills regarding the kinds of activities involved, in terms of whether they involve an interlocutor (= dialogic) or not (= monologic). Furthermore, I think that in terms of the OPI (Oral Proficiency Interview), one is not dealing with or evaluating simply the speaking skill but rather the dialogic skills of speaking as well as listening. That is, the skill being evaluated is not "speaking" alone or "listening" alone but rather a "conversation" skill, which involves dialogic speaking as well as dialogic listening in addition to other aspects of interlocution that do not fall under either speaking or listening, such as understanding cues for turn taking, for showing involvement in a conversation, and so on. Once a dialogic function of the speaking and listening skills has been delimited, it is possible to define and delimit a monologic function for each of these as well: for speaking, this might be defined as speech, which involves little or no interruption or interlocutor, as might be found in a more formal setting involving presentations or the like, while for listening, a monologic function might be defined as intensive listening, which involves little or no interaction, as might be found in overhearing conversations, listening to news broadcasts, or viewing films. Redefining skills in this fashion also allows us to fine-tune evaluations of proficiency in a language of high variability such as Arabic.

With these redefinitions in mind, table 2 summarizes the application of a proficiency-oriented methodology to this linguistic potpourri, which in Arabic reveals a split in the way the skills line up with the possible variants, reflecting Ferguson's classic definition of a diglossic language situation: the (monologic) reading and writing skills are most commonly carried out using MSA, while the dialogic speaking and listening skills (or "conversation") are more commonly associated with a colloquial variant. The skills are listed under each type based on their relative "appropriateness" for each or for the frequency with which one might use the skill given that particular variety. For example, conversational skills (dialogic speaking and listening) are most commonly carried out in a dialect and, while there are occasions when conversation may occur in MSA, its venues are highly restricted to academic, religious, and certain media contexts. On the reverse side, while there are occasions when reading and writing in a dialect are performed, these are highly restricted (to songs, plays, and increasingly blogs) since most reading and writing is done using MSA (although this does vary from country to country, with Egypt and Lebanon showing much higher degrees of the use of written colloquial than other Arab countries).

In addition to these facts about Arabic and how the different skills line up with the different linguistic varieties, there is an additional issue in the way proficiency-oriented testing is heavily skewed toward testing the speaking skill, or what I would rather term the conversational skills (dialogic speaking and listening), through the oral proficiency interview framework. While there are guidelines for proficiency testing in the other three skills, relatively little attention or effort has been expended in developing materials for testing in those areas in comparison to the attention and effort expended on testing the speaking skill. When applied to a context of linguistic variability as found in Arabic, this skewing toward the speaking skill in the evaluation process has had the effect of distorting the relative importance of conversational skills in the overall curriculum of L2 learning and, hence, of the relative importance of including a dialect in the curriculum at the earliest stages.

It is important that the above suggestion (i.e., that the drive for the inclusion of a dialect in the earliest curriculum is due in part to the great importance accorded to the OPI in the evaluation process) not be misunderstood: I am not arguing against such a curriculum but rather for the possibility of other curricula that follow different paths, that stress the need for a more balanced approach among the skills, and that seek to address in a more nuanced fashion issues related to linguistic dissonance and linguistic choice.

Part of the issue involved in the oral proficiency evaluation process is the imposition of a testing model that presupposes a kind of linguistic unity that does not exist

Table 2. Arabic Variation and the "Four" Skills

	MSA	Colloquial
↑	reading (monologic)	conversational (dialogic speaking & listening)
	writing (monologic) listening (monologic)	listening (monologic)
more appropriate	. . .	. . .
less appropriate	. . .	. . .
↓	speaking (monologic) conversational (dialogic speaking & listening)	reading (monologic) writing (monologic)

in Arabic. That is, current and proposed models of testing oral proficiency in Arabic do not reflect the kind of linguistic reality that learners of Arabic experience, although it may well reflect the kind of reality that native speakers of Arabic intuitively experience—namely, that their "Arabic" is a seamless whole in which linguistic variation is a natural part of their various social contexts. This is the kind of intuition that nonnative learners of Arabic should aspire to, and it should be a part of the evaluation at the higher levels of proficiency. Integrating it into a curriculum of Arabic L2 learning requires careful consideration of how best to avoid engendering dissonance in learners at the earliest levels as well as how best to foster the integration of the varieties at the higher levels of proficiency.

At the moment, current evaluation tools for Arabic do not reflect these kinds of issues, in part because to actually handle them, one would need to complicate the process somewhat. That is, if one were to handle the issues of linguistic variation and choice in a fashion that reflects linguistic reality, one should have OPI testing available in each of the varieties at the earliest levels, with a scale that assumes an increasing level of integration of the varieties at the higher levels of proficiency. On the other side of the issue, proficiency in reading texts in a dialect, or in understanding (= listening skill) multiple dialects should be made a part of the higher-level evaluation procedures for reading and listening. In sum, evaluation procedures should reflect the wide variation in the Arabic linguistic sphere and should reflect and support best practices in the pedagogical sphere. They should not be the determining factor in what we teach and how we teach it.

Appendix: Comparative Overview of Arabic Dialects

Table A1. Phonology: Historical Reflexes (vs. Synchronic Borrowing Reflexes in [. . .], and Dialectal Variants in {. . .})

الفصحى	*Fuṣḥā*	Morocco	Egypt	Levantine	Iraq	الفصحى	*Fuṣḥā*	Morocco	Egypt	Levantine	Iraq
ب	b					ر	r				
ف	f					س	s				
م	m					ز	z				
و	w					ش	š				
ث	θ	t	t [s]	t	t	ص	ṣ				
ذ	δ	d	d [z]	δ, d		ك	k				k/č
ظ	δ̣	ḍ	ḍ [ẓ]	ḍ {δ̣}	ḍ	ق	Q	q	ʼ{g}	ʼ{q/k/g}	g
ت	t					أ	ʼ	Ø/y	ʼ/Ø y	ʼ/Ø/y	ʼ/Ø/y
د	d					ح	ḥ				
ض	ḍ				δ̣	خ	x				
ط	ṭ					ع	ʻ				
ج	ǧ		g {ǧ, d}		{y}	غ	ġ				
ي	y					هـ	h				

Table A2. Verbal Inflection تصريف الفعل

الفصحى			Morocco	Egypt	Levantine	Iraq	الفصحى			Morocco	Egypt	Levantine	Iraq
3	كَتَبَ	katab-a	kteb	katab	katab	kitab	3	يَكْتُبُ	ya-ktub-u	ye-kteb	ya-ktib	ye-ktob	yi-ktib
	كَتَبَتْ	katab-at	kteb-et (masha-t)	katab-it	katb-et	kitb-at		تَكْتُبُ	ta-ktub-u	t(e)-kteb	ti-ktib	te-ktob	ti-ktib
2	كَتَبْتَ	katab-ta	kteb- ti	katab-t	katab-t	ki*tab*-it	2	تَكْتُبُ	ta-ktub-u	t(e)-kteb	ti-ktib	te-ktob	ti-ktib
	كَتَبْتِ	katab-ti	kteb- ti	katab-ti	katab-ti	kitab-ti		تَكْتُبِينَ	ta-ktub-īna	t(e)-kteb-ī	ti-ktib-ī	te-ktob-ī	ti-kitb-**<u>īn</u>**
1	كَتَبْتُ	katab-tu	kteb- t	katab-t	katab-t	ki*tab*-it	1	أَكْتُبُ	'a-ktub-u	**<u>n(e)-kteb</u>**	'a-ktib	'a-ktob	'a-ktib
3	كَتَبَا	katabā					3	يَكْتُبَانِ	ya-ktub-āni				
	كَتَبَتَا	katabatā						تَكْتُبَانِ	ta-ktub-āni				
2	كَتَبْتُمَا	katab-tumā					2	تَكْتُبَانِ	ta-ktub-āni				
3	كَتَبُوا	katab-ū	kteb-u	katab-u	katab-u	kitab-aw	3	يَكْتُبونَ	ya-ktub-ūna	ye-kteb-u	yi-ktib-u	ye-ktob-u	yi-kitb-**<u>ūn</u>**
	كَتَبْنَ	katab-na						يَكْتُبْنَ	ya-ktub-na				
2	كَتَبْتُم	katab-tum	kteb-tiw	katab-tu	katab-tu	kitab-tu	2	تَكْتُبونَ	ta-ktub-ūna	t(e)-kteb-u	ti-ktib-u	te-ktob-u	ti-kitb-**<u>ūn</u>**
	كَتَبْتُنَّ	katab-tunna						تَكْتُبْنَ	ta-ktub-na				
1	كَتَبْنا	katab-nā	kteb-na	katab-na	katab-na	kitab-na	1	نَكْتُبُ	na-ktub-u	n(e)-kteb-u	ni-ktib	ne-ktob	ni-ktib

Table A3. Derivation اشتقاق الأفعال

Form	الفصحى		Morocco	Egypt	Levantine	Iraq
I	كَتَبَ	*kataba*	*kteb*	*katab*	*keteb*	*kitab*
II	كَتَّبَ	*kattaba*	*ketteb*	*kattib*	*kattab*	*kattab*
III	كاتَبَ	*kātaba*	*kateb*	*kātib*	*kātab*	*kātab*
IV	أَكْتَبَ	*'aktaba*	*'aktb*	(borrowed)	(borrowed)	(borrowed)
V	تَكَتَّبَ	*takattaba*	*tkttb*	*'itkattib* *ikkattib*	*tkattab*	*tkattab* *kkattab*
VI	تَكاتَبَ	*takātaba*	*tkatb*	*'itkātib* *'ikkātib*	*tkātab*	*tkātab* *kkātab*
VII	اِنْكَتَبَ	*'inkataba*	*nktb* ***'intektab*** ***tenktab***	*'inkatab*	*nkatab*	*nkitab*
VIII	اِكْتَتَبَ	*'iktataba*	*ktatb*	***'itkatab*** *'iktatab*	*ktatab*	*ktitab*
X	اِسْتَكْتَبَ	*'istaktaba*	*stktb*	*'istaktib* ***'istakātib***	*staktab*	*staktab*

Table A4. Syntactic Structures تراكيب نحوية

	الفصحى	Morocco	Egypt	Levantine	Iraq
negation: verbal nonverbal	 ما \ لا \ لم ليس	*ma. . . . . š* ***maš***	*ma. . . . . š* ***miš/muš***	*ma* ***mu***	*ma* ***mu***
analytic genitives	—	*dyal/d-*	*bitā'*	*taba'*	*māl*
relative pronouns	الذي، التي . . .	***dī/eddi***	*'illi*	*halli/yalli*	*'illi*
question words	S-initial	S-initial	**non-S-initial**	S-initial	S-initial
demonstratives	pre-N	pre-N	post-N	pre-N (or post-N)	pre-N (or post-N)
verb prefixes: present: future:	 — سوف \ سـ . . .	 *ka-* *ġadi /ġad-*	 *bi-* *ḥa-*	 *('am) bi-* *rāḥ*	 *da-* *rāḥ*
object marker	إيا			*-yyā-*	*'iyyā-*

Lexical Differences اختلافات معجمية

Table A5. Interrogatives أدوات الاستفهام

	الفصحى	Morocco	Egypt	Levantine	Iraq
who?	مَن	*škun* *(-man)*	*mīn*	*mīn*	*minu* *(-man)*
what?	ما \ ماذا				
	('ayyu šay'in huwa→)	*šnu* *'aš*	*'ē*	*šū*	*šinu* *'ēš* (prep.) *š-* (bef. verb)
which?	أيّ	*šmen // -na*	*'anhu*		*yāhu*
when?	متى	*fuqaš //waqteš*	*'imta*	*ēmta/ēmtīn*	*yamta*
where?	أينَ	*fayn*	*fēn*	*wēn/fēn*	*wayn*
why?	لماذا	*'laš*	*lēh*	*lēš*	*layš/'ilwayš*
how?	كَيْفَ	*kifaš*	*'izzayy*	*kīf*	*šlōn* *kēf/čēf*
how many?	كَم	*šḥal*	*kām*	*kam*	*kamm/čamm*
how much?	كَم	*šḥal*	*'addi 'ē*	*'addēš*	*šgadd*
(yes/no)	هل \ أ	*waš*	—	——	—

Table A6. Questions أسئلة

	الفصحى	Morocco	Egypt	Levantine	Iraq
Who are you?	من أنت؟	*škun nta*	*'inta mīn*	*mīn 'inte*	*(minu 'inta)*
What's your name?	ما اسمُكَ؟	*šnu smiyytak*	*'ismak 'ē*	*šu-smak*	*š-ismak*
What are you doing?	ماذا تعمل؟	*šnu katdīr*	*biti'mil 'ēh*	*šu bte'mal*	*ši-tsawwi*
Why did you go?	لماذا ذهبتَ؟	*'alaš mašīt*	*ruḥt lēh*	*lēš ruḥit*	
When will she come?	متى سَتَجيء؟	*fuqaš ġa-dzi*	*ḥatīgi 'imta*	*'emta raḥ tīji*	*yamta raḥ tiji'*
Where do you live?	أين تَسْكُن؟	*fayn katskun*	*sākin fēn*	*wēn sākin*	*wayn* _____
How did you do it?	كيف عملـتَهُ؟	*kifaš dirt-u*	*'amalt-u 'izzāy*	*kīf 'amilt-o*	
How are you?	كيف حالُكَ؟	*š-xbarek*	*'iz-zayyak*	*kīfak*	*šlōnak/-ič*
How much do you want?	كَم تُريدُ؟	*(šḥal tibġi)*	*'āwiz 'add^{i} 'ēh*	*'addēš biddak*	*šgadd tirīd*
How long have you been here?	كم مضى عليك هنا؟	*šḥal w-intina hnaya*	*ba'ālak 'add 'ēh hina*	*'addēš ṣar-lak hōn*	
What time is it?	كم الساعة؟	*šḥal fessa'a*	*'isssā'a kam*	*'addēš 'issā 'a*	
What do you want?	ماذا تريد؟	*šnu bġiti*	*'āyiz 'ēh*	*šu biddak* *šu trīd*	*ši-trīd*
What's this?	ما هذا؟	*šnu hada*	*'ēh da*	*šu hāda*	
What happened?	ماذا حَدَثَ؟	*šnu wqa'*	*gara 'ēh*	*šu ṣār*	*š-ṣār*

Table A7. Demonstratives and time/place adverbs أسماء إشارة وظروف زمنية

	الفصحى	Morocco	Egypt	Levantine	Iraq
this	هذا	*had/hada*	*da*	*ha/hāda*	*hāδa*
	هذه	*hadi*	*di*	*ha/hādi*	*hāδi/hay*
	هؤلاء	*hadu*	*dōl*	*ha/hadōl*	*(ha) δōl(a)*
that	ذلك	*hadak*	*dukha*	*hadāk*	*(ha)δāk(a)*
	تلك	*hadik*	*dikha*	*hadīk*	*(ha)δīk(a)*
	أولئك	*haduk*	*dukhum*	*hadulak*	*(ha)δōl(ak)*
What's this?	ما هذا؟	*šnu hada*	*'ēh da*	*šu hayda*	*šinu hāδa*
These are my children	هؤلاء أولادي	*hadu wladi*	*dōl wilādi*	*hadōl wilādi*	
this man/book	هذا الرجل	*had l-ktab*	*'irrāgil da*	*harrijjāl*	
now	الآن	*daba*	*dilwa'ti*	*halwa't, halla*	*hassa*
this year	هذه السنة	*hada ssana*	*'issanā-di*	*hassane*	
yesterday	أمسِ	*lbarḥ*	*'imbāriḥ*		*'ilbārḥa*
today	الـيَـوْم	*lyum*	*'innaharḍa*	*lyōm*	*'ilyōm*
tomorrow	غداً	*ġdda*	*bukra*		*bāčir*
here	هُنا	*huna/hnaya*	*hina*	*hōn*	*hina*
there	هناك	*hunāka /tina*	*hināk*	*hināk/honīk*	*hināk*

Table A8. Common Lexical Items كلمات مألوفة

	الفصحى	**Morocco**	**Egypt**	**Levantine**	**Iraq**
want	أرادَ—يُريدُ	*bġa (bġīt)*	*ʿāyiz*	*bidd-(ī)*	*ʾarād/yirīd*
must	يَجِبُ	*xeṣṣ-(ni)*	*lāzim*	*lāzim*	
come	جاء—يجيء	*za/ʾaji*	*geh*		*ja*
go	ذَهَبَ	*mša*	*rāḥ*	*rāḥ*	*rāḥ*
become	أصبح، صار	*ṣbḥ*	*baʾa*	*ṣār*	*ṣār*
happen	حَدَثَ،حَصَلَ	*ṭra*	*ḥaṣal/gara*	*ṣār*	*ṣār*
speak	تكلّم	*tkellim*	*kallim/yikallim*	*ḥaka/ yiḥki*	*ḥiča/yiḥči*
stay	بَقيَ	*gls*	*ʾaʿad*		*biqa/yibqa*
begin	بدأ	*bda*	*ʾibtada*	*ballish*	
give	أعْطى	*ʿṭa*	*ʾidda*	*ʾiʿṭa*	*nṭa*
take	أخَذَ	*xda/čibn*	*xad*		*ʾaxað*
keep on	ظلّ	*tmm/bqa/zid*	*fiḍil/ʾa ʿad*		*ḍall*
good	جيّد	*mezyan*	*kwayyis*	*mnīḥ*	*zayn*
bad	سيّء	*mfillis/qbiḥ*	*wiḥiš*	*ʿāṭil*	*dūni*
thing	شَيئ	*ḥaja*	*ḥāga*	*šē*	*šī*
like	مِثْل	*ki/bḥal*	*zayy*	*mitil*	*miθil*
because	لأنّ	*ʿla qibal*	*ʿašān*	*liʾanno*	*liʾann*
for the sake of	بِسَبَبِ	*ʾila ḥsab*	*ʿašān*	*minšān*	
there is there is no	ثَمّة	*kayn* *ma-kayn-ši*	*fī* *ma-fī-š*	*fī* *ma-fī*	*ʾāku* *mā-ku*
very	جدًّا	*bizaf, blaqyas*	*ʾawi, giddan*	*kitīr*	*kulliš*
still	ما زالَ	*baqi (baqya)*	*lissa*	*baʿd(o)*	*baʿad(o)*
like this	هكذا	*fḥal hadi*	*kida*	*hēk*	
isn't it so?	أليس كذلك؟	*maši hayda*	*miš kida*	*mu hēk/ma hēk*	

Note

1. Munther Younes, *The Integrated Approach to Arabic Instruction* (New York: Routledge, 2015), viii + 58 pp., references, index. ISBN: 978-113822320. Paperback, $20.95.

References

Abboud, P., R. Allen, M. Alosh, P. Heath, C. Kilean, G. Lampe, E. McCarus, F. Mustafa, and D. Parkinson. 1989. "ACTFL Arabic Proficiency Guidelines." *Foreign Language Annals* 22: 373–92.

ACTFL Proficiency Guidelines. 2012. Arabic. https://www.actfl.org/publications/guidelines-and-manuals/actfl-proficiency-guidelines-2012/arabic.

Alhawary, M. T. 2013. "Arabic Second Language Research and Second Language Teaching: What the Teacher, Textbook Writer, and Tester Need to Know." *Al-'Arabiyya* 46: 23–35.

Bishai, Wilson. 1966. "Modern Inter-Arabic." *Journal of the American Oriental Society* 86, no. 3: 319–23.

Blanc, H. 1960. "Stylistic Variation in Spoken Arabic: A Sample of Interdialectal Conversation." In *Contributions to Arabic Linguistics*, ed. C. Ferguson, 81–156. Cambridge, MA: Center for Middle EasternStudies, and Harvard University Press.

Brustad, K., M. al-Batal, and A. Al-Tonsi. 2011. *Al-Kitāb fī Taʿallum al-ʿArabiyya: A Textbook for Beginning Arabic, Part 1*, 3rd ed. Washington, DC: Georgetown University Press.

Ferguson, C. 1959. "Diglossa." *Word* 15: 325–40.

Klibi-Séassau, I., F. Mlih, C. Primus, Ba. Tahhan, and Br. Tahhan. 2007. *Kullo Tamam, Tout va bien: Arabe niveau*, vol. 2. Paris: Delagrave.

Mughazy, Mustafa. 2004. *Dardasha: Let's Speak Egyptian Arabic: A Multidimensional Approach to the Teaching and Learning of Egyptian Arabic as a Foreign Language*. Madison: University of Wisconsin Press and National African Language Resource Center.

Parkinson, Dilworth. 1991. "Searching for Modern Fusha: Real-Life Formal Arabic." *Al-'Arabiyya* 24: 31–64.

Woidich, Manfred. 2004. *kullu tamam! An Introduction to Egyptian Colloquial Arabic*. Cairo: American University in Cairo Press.

Phonetic Correlates of Diglossic and Style Shifting in Arabic

■

Thomas A. Leddy-Cecere, Bennington College

In analyzing Arabic diglossia, researchers have often viewed phonetic/phonological variation between dialectal Arabic (DA) and Modern Standard Arabic (MSA) as a change in style linked to formality or care in speech. This study investigates whether gradient phonetic properties distinguish DA and MSA independently of the phonetic correlates of change across the Labovian stylistic continuum. Two speakers of Egyptian Arabic and two of Syrian Arabic recorded interviews consisting of free speech, a reading passage, and a word list, replicated once each in DA and MSA. Tokens of /a:/were measured for quantity, quality, and dispersion. Analyses of variance (ANOVAs) identified consistent main effects for Labovian style across all speakers. Regarding diglossic register, however, the Syrian speakers showed significant effects not evidenced by the Egyptian speakers. This finding of dialect-specific, differential operation of style versus diglossic shifting argues strongly for the identification of the latter as a separate phenomenon involving switching between two distinct sets of phonetic norms.

Key words: Diglossia, style, register, sociophonetics, intraspeaker variation, Modern Standard Arabic, Egyptian Arabic, Syrian Arabic

Introduction

Previous phonologically oriented examinations of Arabic diglossia (Schmidt 1974; Schulz 1981; Suleiman 1985; Haeri 1996) have centered on categorical differences in the realization of consonantal phonemes; additionally, they have tended to treat as given that the production of acrolectal diglossic forms is the direct result of a change in style, in the traditional meaning of formality or care in speech (see Labov 1972). My goal in the present study is to instead examine gradient phonetic differences between dialectal and Modern Standard Arabic productions and to determine whether such differences exist independently of the phonetic correlates of shift in speech style.

Arabic is consistently referred to as a prototypical example of a diglossic language, a fact that reflects its prominent status in Charles Ferguson's seminal (1959) description of the phenomenon. Across the Arabic-speaking world, dozens of native dialects (hereafter DA) exist in a diglossic relationship with Modern Standard Arabic (MSA), a contemporary code with a basis in the norms of Classical Arabic and acquired primarily through schooling and exposure to media and other cultural material. By traditional accounts, the dialects represent speakers' mother tongues and are the default languages of daily living, while MSA is associated with literacy, officialdom, and gravitas (Bassiouney 2009; Versteegh 2014). Attempts at a purely situational (Ferguson 1959) or interspeaker (Badawi 1973) account of the distribution of diglossic forms have been contested by subsequent scholarship (for discussion, see Bassiouney 2009; Albirini 2016); more recent authors generally choose to view the differences between DA and MSA productions as linked to style, essentially identifying MSA features with Allan Bell's (1984) "deviant hyperstyle variables," though unfortunately few show fidelity to Bell's analytic nuance by choosing to define style as anything beyond a unidimensional continuum of formality (Walters 1996). The bulk of studies into morphosyntactic and lexical variability between DA and MSA display this co-identification of diglossic and stylistic variation, including influential works by Dilworth Parkinson (1993), Guvnor Mejdell (2006), and Abdulkafi Albirini (2016), which explicitly do not differentiate between the two. Typical is the following statement by Parkinson that MSA is "experienced by its users as . . . the upper end of their style spectrum, as opposed to experiencing it as a separate form" (1993, 71).

The few existing studies of phonetic variation in Arabic diglossia, such as those undertaken by Richard Schmidt (1974), David Schulz (1981), and Nilofar Haeri (1996) in Egypt and Saleh Suleiman (1985) in Jordan, are largely consistent with this more prominent tradition in adopting a paradigm that conflates variation in style and diglossic register. Their methodology has consisted primarily of tracking the relative use of DA/MSA phonological variables across more and less formal stylistic situations defined along largely Labovian criteria, and they most often take as their unit of analysis categorical (not gradient) differences in the realization of consonantal segments (e.g., */q/> [q] ~ [ʔ]; */θ, ð, ðˤ/> [θ, ð, ðˤ] ~ [s, z, zˤ]). Research on such classically recognized "diglossic variables," to follow Haeri's terminology, has historically eclipsed other lines of sociophonetic research in Arabic despite a number of analytical limitations. The extreme phonetic salience of such variables is perhaps attractive to researchers but by the same token limits the generalizability of their observed treatment to the rest of the linguistic system (see Trudgill 1986; Schilling-Estes 2002). Additionally, the binary nature of their reported variability restricts analyses to relative rates of occurrence rather than acoustic examinations of noncategorical differences in phonetic character.

In this study, I extend the examination of Arabic diglossia to gradient phonetic properties by examining intraspeaker variation in the production of the phoneme /aː/ in both DA and MSA across the three classic Labovian style contexts of free speech, reading passage, and word list, evaluating tokens along the three parameters of quantity, quality, and dispersion. In so doing, I investigate whether such properties serve to distinguish DA and MSA in a manner distinct from the potential variation of the same variables along the Labovian stylistic continuum. Should this be the case, it will argue strongly for the disentangling of diglossic and stylistic effects in the analysis of sociolinguistic behavior.

Methods

Participants

Four native speakers of Arabic took part in the study; two are speakers of Egyptian Arabic (E1 and E2) and two of Syrian Arabic (S1 and S2). All are female, aged twenty-seven to thirty-five, and are recipients of postgraduate education. Speaker E1, thirty years of age at the time of recording, is a native of Alexandria, Egypt; she completed her education through the master's level in Egypt in the field of English literature and, when recorded, was pursuing a master's degree in Arabic literature at a US university. Speaker E2, thirty-five years old, was born and raised in Cairo, Egypt, where she completed her education through the undergraduate level in the teaching of English as a foreign language. She later earned a master's degree in the United States and began PhD work at a second US university in Arabic language pedagogy, which she was continuing at the time of participation in the study. Speaker S1, twenty-seven years old, is a native of Latakia, Syria, and there earned a bachelor's degree in the field of English literature before coming to the United States and beginning a master's degree in Middle Eastern studies. Speaker S2, thirty-two years old, of Damascus, Syria, completed her education through the master's level at a Syrian university in Arabic language pedagogy. All participants were employed as teachers of Arabic as a foreign language at a major US university and, as part of their teaching duties, were accustomed to producing extended, extemporaneous discourse in MSA on a day-to-day basis. When recorded, the four participants were all residing in a major city in Texas and had been resident in the United States for 7 months (S1), 2 years (E1), 3.5 years (S2), and 5 years (E2).

The comparatively small number of participants available to take part in the study motivated the choice to design a sample relatively homogeneous along several prominent demographic parameters, including age, gender, education level, and professional exposure to MSA. While such homogeneity obviously places limits on the generalizability of the study's results across the broader Arabic-speaking population, it simultaneously controls for the presence of several recognized factors in the conditioning of linguistic variation that might otherwise obscure the interpretation of findings from a sample of this size.

Procedure and Materials

Participants were interviewed one-on-one, three in private offices and the fourth in a private dwelling. Each interview consisted of two halves, each containing three parallel components. The first half of the interview was conducted in the speakers' native DA, the second half in MSA; this was explicitly requested in the interview instructions, accompanied by the switch of the interviewer himself to use of the desired diglossic register. The DA portion of the interview was conducted first in all cases to prevent any performative keying associated with MSA use from carrying over to subsequent parts of the interview in which the DA register would be desired (see Brustad 2017); this concern incidentally overruled the implementation of a counterbalancing experimental design. The interviewer (the author) is known to all informants to approximately equal degrees and is a proficient nonnative speaker of Egyptian Arabic and MSA, the former of which he spoke during the DA halves of all interviews. Although the potential for differential accommodative influence on the production of the Syrian Arabic speakers is thus recognized, it shall be seen that no direct evidence of such is furnished by the study's results.

The three components repeated in each half were a free-speech interview session, a reading passage, and a word list. During the free interview sessions, participants provided a basic self-introduction, speaking for approximately eight minutes in each half about their upbringings, family members, educations, and professional lives. DA reading passages of approximately 250 words were prepared and set in Arabic script by two nonparticipating native speakers of the dialects involved in the study and consisted of a self-introduction for a fictional character, thereby maintaining a broad continuity of topic with the free-speech material;[1] similarly, MSA reading passages of comparable length were selected from a collection of first-person self-introductions composed by Arab novelists for inclusion in an encyclopedia of modern Arab authors. To avoid issues of regional differences in MSA standards, the Syrian participants read a passage written by a Syrian author; the Egyptian participants, one by an Egyptian author. Word lists for each dialect and MSA were compiled using dictionary sources (Wehr and Cowan 1994; Hinds and Badawi 1986; Stowasser and Ani 2004) and contained thirty target items plus ten distractors, with lexemes specifically selected to belong unambiguously to either DA or MSA. Compared to previous work, the present study is innovative in not presuming an a priori restriction of the written domain to MSA and replicating all tasks in both register conditions. Word lists and reading passages in all varieties are included in the appendix. Interviews were recorded in a quiet setting using a Tascam DR-100mkII recorder with a Shure dynamic headset microphone.

Measures and Analysis

Following recording, tokens of stressed /a:/were identified and manually marked in Praat (v. 5.4.02). The phoneme /a:/ was selected as the target of analysis because of its gradient phonetic nature, its frequency, and the author's perception through previous observation that it would represent a significant locus of variation. After collection and tagging, a script was used to extract values for the duration and the midpoint first through third formant frequencies of all tokens of /a:/. Total token counts ranged between 286 and 421 per speaker (avg. 366).

In order to account for potential global differences in speech rate across interview components (see Thomas 2011), the measure for quantity of /a:/ was not duration in milliseconds but rather the ratio of the length of /a:/ tokens to the mean length of /a/ tokens drawn from the same interview component (e.g., DA free speech, MSA word list); this technique is modeled on that used in Mohamed Embarki's (2007) investigation of vowel quantity in Moroccan Arabic. Following the findings of Kenneth de Jong and Bushra Adnan Zawaydeh (2002) and the predictions of Ian Maddieson (1985), steps were taken to control for the effect of syllable structure and consonant environment on vowel length: only tokens of /a:/ and /a/ in open syllables and preceding voiced consonants (consistently the most numerous subset across all participants) were used in these calculations. Additionally, tokens adjacent to the glides /w, j/ were excluded as the high degree of coarticulation complicated the consistent identification of the vowel onset/offset. A consequence of these phonetic constraints was to similarly restrict the morphological variability of tokens, as together they conspire to rule out the vast majority of inflectional affixal elements containing /a(ː)/ in the Arabic varieties examined; as such, no affixal tokens were included in measures of quantity.

The measures for quality consist of the F1 and F2 values (in Hz) for each token. These were considered separately to more precisely reveal the locus of any observed phonetic differentiation as well as to provide direct comparability to previous phonetic studies of Arabic reporting a similar level of detail (e.g., de Jong and Zawaydeh 2002). The front and back allophones [æː] and [ɑː] (conditioned by consonantal environment) were distinguished in coding to allow for the investigation of potential interactions between allophonic realization and the other factors being examined.

The measure of dispersion is defined as the Euclidean distance of each token from the center of the vowel space delimited by the allophones [æː ~ ɑː]. The mean F1 and F2 values were calculated for both [æː] and [ɑː] in each of the given speaker's six interview components; the midpoint between these means was then calculated on the F2 × F1 coordinate plane (i.e., $[\mu_{F2}, \mu_{F1}]$). The Euclidean distance from each individual token to the relevant midpoint was then calculated using the formula $\sqrt{(x_1 - x_2)^2 + (y_1 - y_2)^2}$, delivering a measure in hertz. These values were included among the study's measures in accordance with crosslinguistic observations of the "stretching" of articulatory and perceptual vowel space across stylistic contexts (Warner 2012); on this basis, it is plausible to hypothesize that such effects might similarly obtain to the space between two allophonic realizations of a single phoneme.

Once appropriate values were calculated for each token using the measures described above, the data were analyzed via a series of factorial ANOVAs carried out in SPSS (v. 20). For each speaker, four ANOVAs were run: one for quantity, one for dispersion, and one each for F1 and F2 to evaluate quality. The tests for quantity and dispersion were of a 3 × 2 design with Interview Element (free speech versus reading passage versus word list) and Register (DA versus MSA) as factors; the quality tests were of a 3 × 2 × 2 design with Interview Element, Register, and Allophone (front versus back) as factors.

Should the traditional equation of diglossic variability with Labovian style shifting prove warranted, it would be expected that any significant main effects or interactions captured by way of these analyses would be observed for the factors of Element and Register in a parallel manner along the progression from free speech to reading passage to word list and from DA to MSA. Should respective effects for Element and Register diverge in the production of the study's speakers, however, this existing hypothesis will be left unsupported and an empirical basis will be provided for the interpretation of diglossic and style shifting as discretely identifiable sociolinguistic phenomena.

Results

Quantity

Quantity data from all four participants, presented in table 1, displayed a main effect for Interview Element (hereafter "Element") to the effect that the ratio of /a:/ durations to /a/ durations was greater in the word-list condition ("L") than it was in the free-speech condition ("F") to a statistically significant degree;[2] some variation existed regarding the distinctness of the reading passage data ("P") from the remaining two conditions. Individual results were E1 ($F_{(2, 101)} = 9.765, p < .001$; F < P, $p < .001$; F < L, $p = .001$),[3] E2 ($F_{(2, 156)} = 30.231, p < .001$; F < P, $p < .001$; F < L, $p < .001$), S1 ($F_{(2, 166)} = 6.378, p = .002$; F < P, $p = .003$; F < L, $p = .016$), and S2 ($F_{(2, 142)} = 9.795, p < .001$; F < L, $p < .001$; P < L, $p = .001$).

The only participant to show a main effect for Register was E2, whose MSA ratios were greater than her DA ratios ($F_{(1, 156)} = 11.303, p = .001$). E1 was the only participant to display a significant interaction between Register and Element ($F_{(2, 101)} = 5.917$, $p = .004$), whereby DA ratios were larger than MSA ones in the F ($p = .013$)[4] and P ($p = .038$) conditions, although smaller to a nearly significant level in the L condition ($p = .091$).

These results show that vowel quantity as calculated in ratio form increases for all speakers as they progress from the least formal pole of the Labovian stylistic continuum to the most formal. The same generalization cannot be made, however, regarding the transition from DA to MSA, as the two effects detected for Register apply to only single speakers on an idiosyncratic and contradictory basis.

Table 1. Means and Standard Deviations of Quantity Results by Interview Element and Diglossic Register (expressed as ratio of /a:/:/a/)

Speaker		Interview Element			Diglossic Register	
		Free Speech	Passage	Word List	DA	MSA
E1	*M*	1.864	2.274	2.257	2.190	2.068
	SD	0.4989	0.4658	0.4051	0.5060	0.4798
E2	*M*	1.733	2.154	2.316	1.855	2.048
	SD	0.4479	0.4509	0.3575	0.5008	0.4816
S1	*M*	1.960	2.314	2.341	2.266	2.074
	SD	0.6672	0.6271	0.5029	0.6278	0.6568
S2	*M*	2.029	2.143	2.622	2.297	2.137
	SD	0.6072	0.5434	0.7146	0.6055	0.6559

Dispersion

Dispersion results are displayed in table 2. A main effect for Element is present for all four speakers such that the dispersion distances for free-speech data are significantly lower than those for word-list data; as for quantity, above, the reading passage data showed some variation as to its distinctness from either or both remaining elements. Individual results were E1 ($F_{(2, 283)} = 7.391, p = .001$; F < L, $p = .001$; P < L, $p = .013$); E2 ($F_{(2, 380)} = 16.683, p < .001$; F < L, $p < .001$; P < L, $p < .001$); S1 ($F_{(2, 418)} = 7.070, p = .001$; F < L, $p = .002$); and S2 ($F_{(2, 371)} = 6.712, p = .001$; F < P, $p = .005$; F < L, $p = .006$).

The two Syrian participants, S1 and S2, showed a significant main effect for Register, with MSA dispersion measures significantly greater than DA measures: S1 ($F_{(1, 419)} = 38.407, p < .001$); and S2 ($F_{(1, 372)} = 7.118, p = .008$). Neither E1 nor E2 showed significant effects for Register, although both provided hints of an opposite trend to S1 and S2 with DA values greater than MSA values, E2 to a marginally nonsignificant degree ($F_{(1, 381)} = 2.751, p = .098$).

The one speaker to show a significant interaction of Element × Register was E2 ($F_{(2, 380)} = 5.240, p = .006$), whose MSA and DA measures were distinct in the word-list condition only ($p < .001$). This distinction operated in the opposite direction from those of S1 and S2, with DA measures greater than MSA.

Similar to vowel quantity, dispersion was observed to significantly increase for all speakers in the progression from free speech to word list on the stylistic continuum. Unlike the quantity measures, however, effects for Register were also readily identifiable. Speakers S1 and S2 both showed an increase in dispersion in the shift from DA to MSA. Participants E1 and E2, however, did not share in this pattern, and in fact a significant opposing interaction was detected in E2's word-list values.

Table 2. Means and Standard Deviations of Dispersion Results by Interview Element and Diglossic Register (in Hz)

Speaker		Interview Element			Diglossic Register	
		Free Speech	Passage	Word List	DA	MSA
E1	*M*	413.8	432.7	500.3	442.8	434.0
	SD	157.4	152.2	101.6	149.3	148.5
E2	*M*	392.3	387.5	499.0	423.0	396.9
	SD	130.3	146.8	139.1	151.3	132.9
S1	*M*	208.5	232.8	268.2	186.5	257.6
	SD	114.3	141.4	113.2	102.4	133.9
S2	*M*	208.2	257.1	271.2	216.6	256.8
	SD	120.7	148.1	154.6	134.0	142.9

Quality: F1 Frequency

Table 3 shows mean results for F1 quality. Participants E2, S1, and S2 all displayed a main effect for Element such that F1 values tended to decrease from free-speech data to reading passage data to word-list data, but the specifics are not as uniform as the results for quantity and dispersion measures. E2 showed a main effect ($F_{(2, 380)}$ = 7.896, $p < .001$) with F > P > L, but in the aggregate none of the three elements were distinct from one another to a statistically significant degree. This appears to be the result of a difference in the behavior of the front and back /a:/allophones in reading passage data: for the front allophones, the free-speech and passage data were distinct from the word list but not one another (F > L, $p = .001$; P > L, $p = .019$), while for the back allophones the reverse is true, with the free-speech data distinct from the word list and very nearly so from the passage but the latter two not distinct from one another (F > L, $p = .041$; F > P, $p = .061$). S1 also showed a main effect for Element ($F_{(2, 485)}$ = 23.681, $p < .001$) with F1 decreasing from free speech to reading passage (F > P, $p < .001$), although her word-list data broke with the patterns of the other three participants by sharply increasing F1 values, thereby not completing the F > P > L progression. Participant S2 showed a main effect for Element as well ($F_{(2, 371)}$ = 4.428, $p = .013$), with the word list significantly less than both other elements (F > L, $p = .001$; P > L, $p = .007$). Participant E1's results for Element did not attain significance but came close to doing so ($F_{(2, 283)}$ = 2.374, $p = .095$) and displayed the same general F > P > L pattern as those of E2 and S2, though not to significant levels.

Participants S1 and S2 showed a main effect for register whereby DA F1 values were globally higher than MSA F1 values: S1 ($F_{(1, 486)}$ = 22.354, $p < .001$), S2 ($F_{(1, 372)}$ = 9.640, $p = .002$). Participant E2 showed a significant effect in the opposite direction, with MSA F1 values greater than the corresponding DA values ($F_{(1, 381)}$ = 6.671,

Table 3. Means and Standard Deviations of F1 Quality Results by Interview Element and Diglossic Register (in Hz)

Speaker		Interview Element			Diglossic Register	
		Free Speech	Passage	Word List	DA	MSA
E1	*M*	687.4	683.3	661.5	682.7	678.1
	SD	94.49	117.8	93.40	111.9	93.03
E2	*M*	692.3	686.6	674.5	675.1	698.2
	SD	89.35	96.86	85.30	100.6	80.80
S1	*M*	736.5	699.0	741.5	732.1	707.6
	SD	76.49	77.42	84.08	80.28	78.13
S2	*M*	857.9	852.8	822.0	861.6	839.6
	SD	73.23	67.26	54.89	74.61	62.31

$p = .010$), while Participant E1's results did not reach significance. No significant interactions were observed that would seem to qualify the interpretation of these main effects.

These results indicate a trend of decreasing F1 values as speakers progressed across the Labovian stylistic continuum, with significant main effects for Element observed in the production of Participants E2, S1, and S2 and E1 showing less conclusive evidence of a similar pattern. Speakers S1 and S2 also showed significant effects for diglossic register whereby DA F1 values were higher than MSA values. This finding, however, was restricted to these two speakers, and Participant E2 in fact showed a significant effect in the opposite direction.

Quality: F2 Frequency

In analysis of the results for F2 quality (shown in table 4), Participant S2 was the only speaker to show a significant main effect for Element ($F_{(2, 371)} = 12.034$, $p < .001$); however, once the interaction between Element and Allophone is taken into account, the picture changes dramatically.

All four speakers displayed a significant interaction whereby the word-list condition displayed the highest F2 values for the front ([æː]) allophones only, though varying somewhat with regard to the distinctness of L from either or both of F and P. Individual results for the Element × Allophone interaction were: E1 ($F_{(2, 283)} =$ 4.150, $p = .017$; F < L, $p = .013$), E2 ($F_{(2, 380)} = 5.225$, $p = .006$; F < L, $p = .001$; P < L, $p = .039$), S1 ($F_{(2, 415)} = 3.569$, $p = .029$; P < L marginally nonsignificant $p = .060$), S2 ($F_{(2, 371)} = 4.628$, $p = .010$; F < P, $p < .001$; F < L, $p < .001$). In order to illustrate these effects, plots of the Element × Allophone interaction are provided for each speaker (figs. 1–4).

Table 4. Means and Standard Deviations of F2 Quality Results by Interview Element and Diglossic Register (in Hz)

Speaker		Interview Element			Diglossic Register	
		Free Speech	Passage	Word List	DA	MSA
E1	*M*	1803	1840	1659	1832	1734
	SD	396.5	409.2	506.7	417.3	439.3
E2	*M*	1980	1925	1756	1937	1922
	SD	305.3	365.4	512.6	386.4	358.3
S1	*M*	1585	1557	1501	1475	1632
	SD	202.4	246.0	282.3	184.1	244.5
S2	*M*	1688	1782	1702	1705	1747
	SD	202.2	245.4	300.3	213.5	262.6

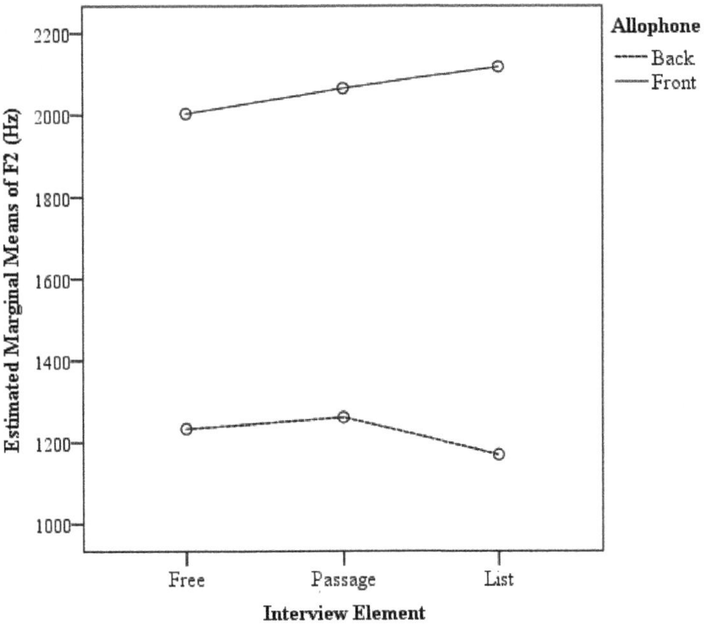

Figure 1. E1 F2 Means (Hz), Element × Allophone

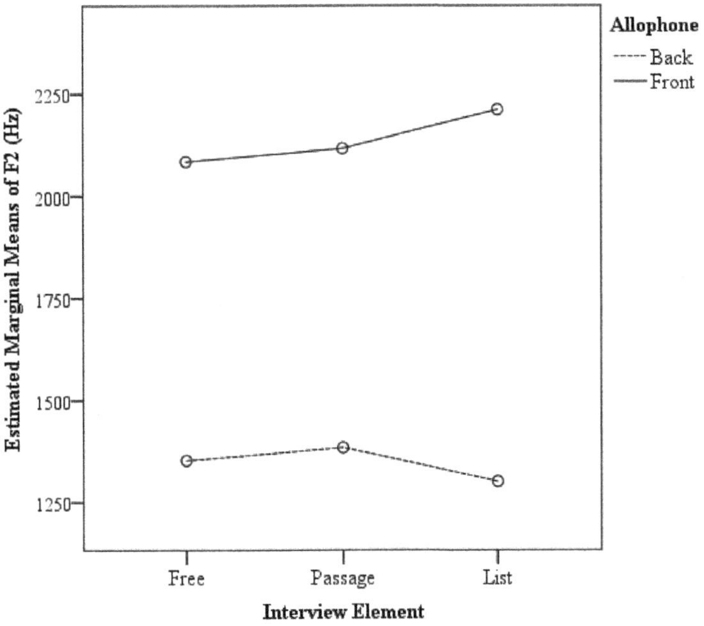

Figure 2. E2 F2 Means (Hz), Element × Allophone

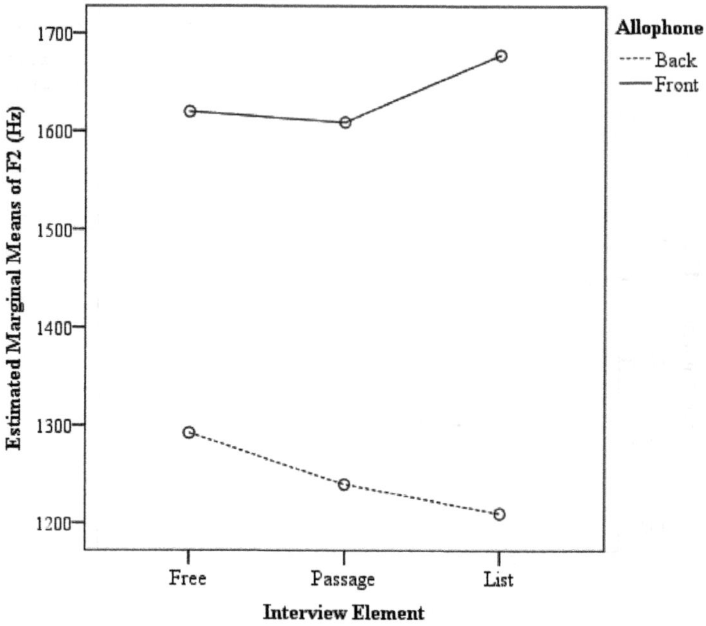

Figure 3. S1 F2 Means (Hz), Element × Allophone

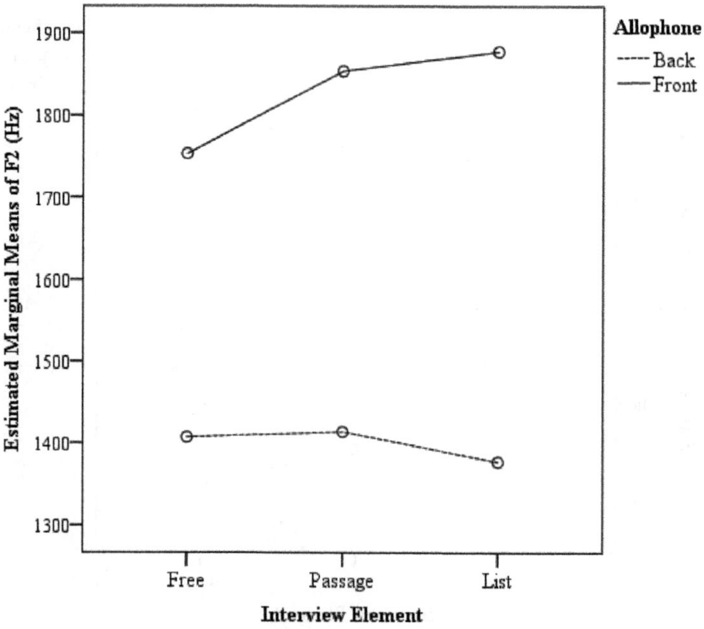

Figure 4. S2 F2 Means (Hz), Element × Allophone

The two Syrian participants, S1 and S2, displayed significant main effects for Register, to the effect that MSA F2 values were greater than DA F2 values: S1 ($F_{(1, 372)} = 6.086, p = .014$) and S2 ($F_{(1, 416)} = 83.700, p < .001$). Significant interactions of Register × Allophone showed these effects to be localized primarily in the front allophones: S1 ($F_{(1, 416)} = 12.912, p < .001$) and S2 ($F_{(1, 372)} = 7.676, p = .006$). Neither of the Egyptian participants E1 and E2 showed significant main effects or interactions. Plots of the Register × Allophone interaction (significant for S1 and S2) are provided in figures 5–8 for comparative purposes.

For all speakers, then, significant interactions were observed such that F2 values of the frontal allophone [æ:] were highest in the word-list condition, representing the most formal pole of the Labovian stylistic continuum. The production of participants S1 and S2 also showed a significant effect for diglossic register, with DA F2 values lower than MSA values. This effect was not mirrored in the speech of E1 and E2, however, who did not show any evidence for a significant effect of diglossic register on the value of F2.

Discussion

For every variable measured, parallel global effects for Element (i.e., Labovian style shift as traditionally defined) were discernable across the production of all four participants. Quantity ratios of /a:/ to /a/ increased as speakers progressed from free-speech to word-list conditions. Dispersion similarly increased. Regarding quality, F1 was observed to lower (marginally nonsignificant for E1, significant for all others) and F2 to rise as speakers progressed along the Labovian stylistic continuum, the change in the latter variable localized in the realization of the front ([æ:]) allophones.[5]

The effects of Register (i.e., diglossic shift[6]), however, were not universal. Rather, they applied differentially to speakers of the two DA dialects examined, Syrian Arabic and Egyptian Arabic. The two speakers of Syrian Arabic displayed increased dispersion measures, lowered F1 values, and heightened F2 values in the shift from DA to MSA (the difference in F2 again primarily enacted in the front allophones); the speakers of Egyptian Arabic did not. This differentiation is not likely to be the simple artifact of a lack of statistical power, as the data from the two Egyptian Arabic speakers in fact tends to present either neutral or opposing numerical trends, rising to statistical significance in the case of E2's F1 values and nearly so in the same speaker's dispersion values.

The conclusion to be drawn from these results is as follows: while the observed effects of change in Labovian speech style obtain ubiquitously across the entire

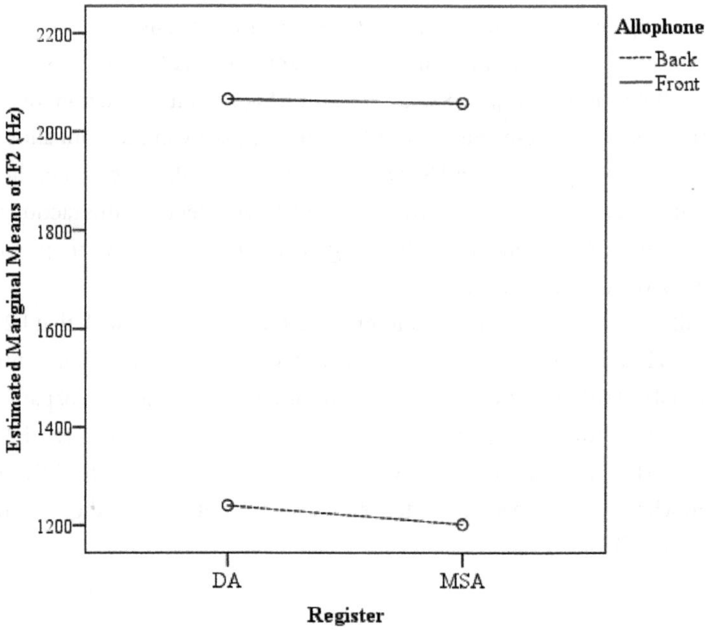

Figure 5. E1 F2 Means (Hz), Register × Allophone

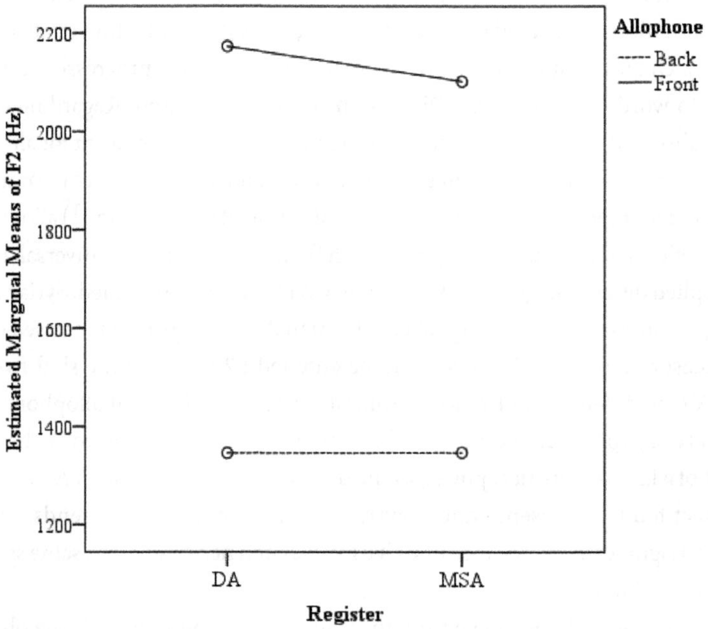

Figure 6. E2 F2 Means (Hz), Register × Allophone

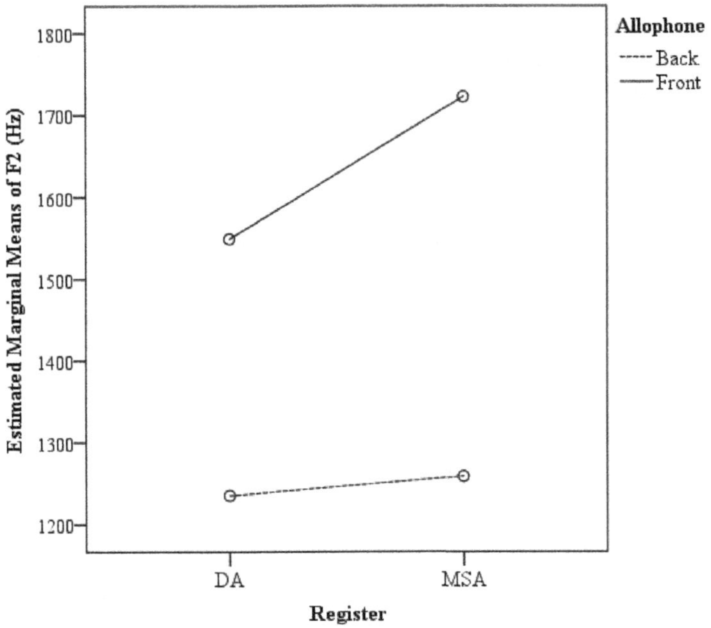

Figure 7. S1 F2 Means (Hz), Register × Allophone

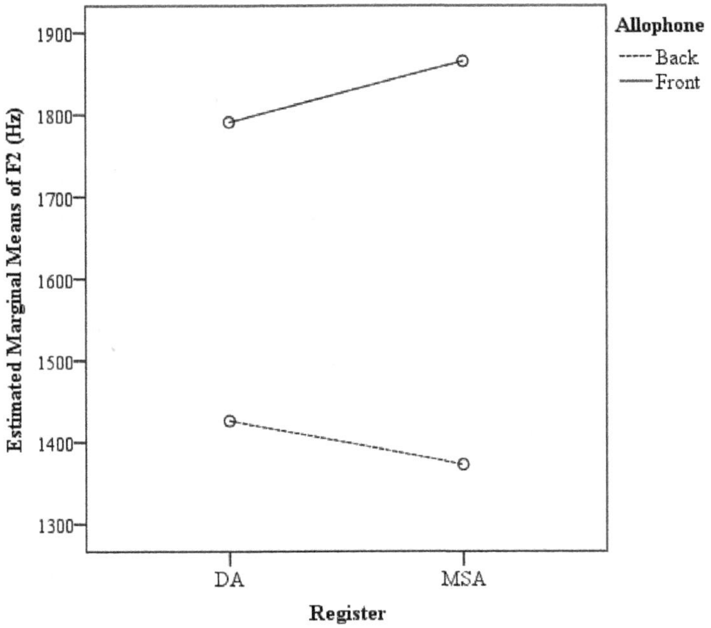

Figure 8. S2 F2 Means (Hz), Register × Allophone

sample population, all non-idiosyncratic effects of change in diglossic register apply only on a dialect-specific basis. This finding of differential operation for style versus diglossic shifting argues strongly for the separate status of the two sets of linguistic phenomena.

Implications and Future Steps

This study's findings clearly contradict the conflation of diglossic and style shifting in Arabic that has typified the interpretations of numerous researchers to date: the phonetic effects of diglossic shifting are not comparable across speakers of Egyptian and Syrian Arabic, as the effects of style shifting appear to be (at least within the confines of a limited sample group). In search of a motivation for this differentiation, the observed uniformity of style shifting effects across the sample raises the question of potential psycholinguistic factors; in this light, it is perhaps noteworthy that some of these same effects (e.g., increases in quantity, dispersion) have been convincingly linked with hyperarticulation phenomena both in Arabic (de Jong and Zawaydeh 2002) and other languages (Brink, Wright, and Pisoni 1998; Harnsberger, Wright, and Pisoni 2008). However, these correspondences are not complete: de Jong and Zawaydeh, for example, found lexical focus to be accompanied by a significant *rise* in F1 among Jordanian Arabic speakers, as opposed to the significant drop associated with style shifting in the current study. The significance of the overlap is thus not altogether clear and awaits input from future, targeted research. Also of potential interest in this regard is the consistently medial yet variably (in)distinct patterning of the reading passage data vis-à-vis the free-speech and word-list values across measures and speakers. While the precise significance of this is difficult to interpret based on the current data alone, it does suggest that the effects observed for style shifting are not the simple product of differences in the spoken versus written mode or connected versus unconnected speech. Precisely which combination of social and psychological factors the Labovian stylistic continuum serves to reflect remains a topic of open debate (see Schilling-Estes 2002; Thomas 2011), but it seems clear that in this circumstance such mechanical considerations of experimental design are not the source, or at least the sole source, of the variation observed.

Regardless of any interplay between sociolinguistic and psycholinguistic underpinnings, what is evident from the present study is that Arabic style shifting and diglossic shifting are not equivalent and must be treated separately in forthcoming analytical approaches. This study's results, however, remain agnostic regarding the potential for a direct or indirect relationship between the two discretely identifiable phenomena. It should not go unnoticed that several of the self-same phonetic trends (increase in dispersion and F2 of [æ:], decrease in F1) that distinguish style differences across all speakers also serve to mark register differences in those participants who display them. It is unknown whether this is indicative of a true causal or structural link between the two shifting types or a mere coincidence due to the specific phonetic properties of /a:/ in each of the relevant dialects involved in the study. Further research involving additional vocalic and consonantal variables would lower the chances of accidental resemblance in this regard and would allow for a more definitive investigation of interrelations between diglossic and style shifting as self-standing phenomena. It similarly goes without saying that future investigation of this study's findings would be bolstered by replication over a larger and more diverse sample, with the comparison of results from members of both genders especially desired given previous findings of gender-based differences in the use of MSA variables (Haeri 1996; Amara, Spolsky, and Tushyeh 1999). Corroboration of the present investigation's results in such a setting would be a significant step toward a novel and nuanced conception of diglossic variability as separate from Labovian style shifting, with implications for the understanding of both phenomena in Arabic and in other languages worldwide.

Appendix: Interview Materials

The written interview materials (consisting of word lists and reading passages) are presented below. The three word lists were compiled from dictionary sources: Egyptian Arabic from Hinds and Badawi (1986), Syrian Arabic from Stowasser and Ani (2004), and Modern Standard Arabic from Wehr and Cowan (1994). The Egyptian Arabic reading passage was composed by Iman Soliman and the Syrian Arabic reading passage by Lama Nassif: in each case, the author's original language and orthography was unaltered, and the passages were presented to participants precisely as shown here. The MSA reading passages were drawn from the anthology *Aʿlām al-Adab al-ʿArabī al-Muʿāṣir* (Campbell 1996): the passage read by Egyptian participants represents a portion of the autobiographical entry by ʿAbd al-Raḥmān al-Abnūdī (pp. 173–74); by Syrian participants, that by Saʿīd Ḥūrāniyyah (pp. 515–16).

Word Lists

Table A1. Egyptian Arabic Word List

راجل	الحاكم دا	اتكسر	ضاني
طازة	باظت	مدابح	حاجة
ابتدى	ستاشر	السنة اللي فاتت	شافه
راسه	بيتخانق	جزمجي	المرادي
واكل	فاكر	النوبادي	حاجاتي
شاطر قوي	مراته	دهبي	بقى
السنادي	جاهز	الليلادي	الرقاصة دي
بحري	بلطجي	حاضر	امبارح
ظابط	انضرب	فاضي	خمستاشر
اندبح	اتكتب	أربعتاشر	حيسافر

Table A2. Syrian Arabic Word List

انضرب	هالحاكم	كذا	شافه
انكسر	صارت	صباطه	خاطر
امبارح	تازة	تلاقي	تاخد
هادا	حابب	حاضر	تقراها
غراضك	حكي	مصاري	ضابط
السنة اللي فاتت	كتير شاطر	رح يسافر	أخد
لكان	قاسي	حاكي	انكتب
مدابح	حدا	دهبي	هراكي
نهار	راسه	كنادر	إصابة
راحت	اندبح	حرس	هالرقاصة

Table A3. Modern Standard Arabic Word List

هذا الحاكم	الزجل	الإفادة	قاض
يتراسل	انفساده	ذابل	اشتراكه
هذه الرقاصة	ثلاثة وثلاثون	عظائم	يفارق
ذئابهم	إنقاذهم	انصرافه	سيسافر
التي	شاطر للغاية	ثماني عشرة	تصادف
إحدى عشرة	مبادئ	متثاقل	متى
السنة التي فاتت	إضرارك	ساذج	أبدا
التفه	احتكاكهم	نماذج	هو نظف
الذي	هو جلس	حادئ	هو حدث
واحد وأربعون	ثقابكم	يخاطب	انضباطه

Reading Passages

EGYPTIAN ARABIC READING PASSAGE

أنا اسمي آمال عندي تلاتين سنة، وباشتغل عاملة نضافة في البنك التجاري الدولي. أنا متجوزة وعندي 3 أولاد. أنا أصلا من مدينة سوهاج ولكن أهلي سافروا المنيا وعشنا هناك سنتين وبعدين والدي الله يرحمه بقى،

جاله شغل في القاهرة واضطرينا نيجي مصر. وقتها كنت في المدرسة الثانوية لكن للأسف ما كملتش تعليمي عشان جالي عريس ووالدي أصر إني اتجوز. كان عندي ستاشر سنة لما اتجوزت .. أيوه كنت صغيرة خالص .. جوزي جاب لي شقة في مدينة العاشر في القاهرة وخلفت على طول .. كنت ساكنة بعيدة عن أمي فطبعا كان علي أعمل كل حاجة لوحدي : الطبيخ والغسيل وتربية الأولاد يعني زي مانتو راسيين على الأمور دي بقى ..

جوزي راجل طيب وبيعاملني كويس وبيخاف على بيته وعياله ، هو موظف في شركة حكومية، دخلِنا محدود طبعا وعشان كدا باشتغل .. عشان أساعد في البيت وأهو زي ما بيقولوا في المثل: "النوايا تسند الزير" أنا بحب ولادي جدا وباشتغل عشان أضمن لهم مستقبل أحسن وحياة مرتاحة مش زي الحياة اللي عايشينها دلوقتي. تامر ابني في سنة ساتسة ابتدائي وسهيلة أخته في سنة خمسة أنا حامل في شهري السابع وبأدعي ربنا يرزقني بولد ويبقى الحمد لله على كدا.

أنا ماليش طلبات المهم الأولاد يكونوا مبسوطين وطلابتهم مقضية، لما اولد هاضطر آخد أجازة من الشغل .. قانون العمل بيديني أجازة وضع .. 90 يوم بعد الولادة بأجر كامل.

عادة أنا ماليش طلبات المهم الأولاد يكونوا مبسوطين .. باحب أطبخ اتفرج على السينما وكل سنة باحب أسافر أحضر المولد في الأقصر .. باقابل أصحابي بتوع زمان وباشوف اعمامي وخالاتي يعني بتبقى فرصة حلوة ولمة جميلة من كل حتة في البلد.

نفسي في ولد يارب يجيني ولد المرا دي . . .

SYRIAN ARABIC READING PASSAGE

أنا اسمي ندى وعمري عشرين سنة. أنا ساكنة بالشام وبدرس بكلية الاقتصاد بجامعة دمشق. أنا ساكنة مع أهلي ببيت بمنطقة المهاجرين. خلقت بالشام وكل عمري عايشة بالشام بس نحنا بالأصل من السويدا. بابا وماما كانوا ساكنين بالسويدا أول ما تجوزوا بس انتقلوا عالشام من واحد وعشرين سنة. البابا بيشتغل بوزارة التعليم العالي وماما أستاذة لغة عربية بمدرسة قريبة من بيتنا. عندي تلات إخوة. أخي الكبير مهندس ميكانيك وهلق عم يدرس الدكتوراة بجامعة مانشيستر ببريطانيا. هو معيد بجامعة دمشق وسافر على بريطانيا من سنتين. كان كتير يساعدني بالرياضيات وأنا صغيرة! أخي التاني طالب ماجستير بجامعة دمشق وعم يدرس إدارة الأعمال. ممكن إدرس نفس الشي لما إتخرج من الجامعة. إختي الصغيرة طالبة بكالوريا وحابة تدرس طب أسنان. طب الأسنان بدها علامات عالية وإن شاء الله إختي تقدر تجيب العلامات المطلوبة. هي شاطرة وما بينخاف عليها وكلنا متوقعين إنها تنجح بتفوق.

أنا هلق بالسنة التالتة بالجامعة وإن شاء الله رح إتخرج السنة الجاية. ما بعرف إذا كان لازم إشتغل بالأول أو إدرس الماجستير. أهلي عم يقولوا إنو أحسن إدرس وبعدين إشتغل بس أنا حابة آخد خبرة عمل بالأول. على كل لسا عندي وقت للتفكير وممكن إسأل أساتذتي كمان.

بوقت فراغي بحب إسمع موسيقى. بحب فيروز كتير ودايماً بسمعها. من أنا وصغيرة بابا وماما كانوا دايماً يسمعوا فيروز وممكن منشان هيك أنا بحب فيروز كل هالقد. ما بتخيل حياتي من دونها! كمان بحب إقرا من الأدب العربي. من الشعراء بحب نزار قباني وجبران خليل جبران. بحس إني بعالم تاني لما بقرالهن. بحب السفر بس بحياتي ما سافرت برا سوريا وبتمنى زور بلاد تانية. إن شاء الله!

MODERN STANDARD ARABIC READING PASSAGE FOR EGYPTIAN PARTICIPANTS

ولدت في قرية أبنود محافظة قنا—جنوب مصر—(الصعيد) عام ١٩٣٨ من أب كان طحاناً في القرية، وحفظ القرآن في القرية، وهرب إلى المدينة ليتمّ تعليمه، وحقّق مركزاً مرموقاً في مدينة قنا بصفته مأذوناً شرعيّاً، ورجل

دين جاد، وشاعراً، وأستاذاً للغة العربية، وإماماً لمسجد سجن المدينة (وهو من أكبر سجون مصر). وصدرت له الفية منظومة في النحو العربي على غرار (الفية ابن مالك) بعنوان النفحات الوهبية في علم العربية وقصيدة طويلة في مديح الرسول تحت عنوان: منحة المنّان في مدح سيّد الذكران عن نهج قصيدة الإمام البوصيري.

ولدت هزيلاً من أمّ أمّية مصابة بالملاريا، وعشت شظف العيش في القرية حيث رعوت الغنم، وجنيت القطن، وعملت في حقول الآخرين.

ذهبنا إلى المدينة للالتحاق بأبي فالتحقت بالكتّاب لأتعلّم القرآن وبالمدرسة الإبتدائيّة.

بعد إتمام دراستي الثانويّة قرّرت العمل، فعملت بالمحاكم لمدة خمس سنوات، كنت خلالها أهتمّ بأغاني الفلّاحين وملاحمهم في قريتي وأحفظها، وبدأت كتابة شعري بلغة أهل قريتي، وعرف شعري طريقه إلى صحف القاهرة.

استقلت من عملي في المحاكم في إحدى الجلسات احتجاجاً على حكم أصدره القاضي.

رحلت إلى القاهرة في فبراير عام ١٩٦٢، ورفضت الالتحاق بأي عمل وأصبحت شاعراً متفرغاً للمرة الأولى في مصر.

كتبت العديد من الأغنيات، وكتبت لمسرح العرائس عدّة مسرحيّات.

في عام ١٩٦٥ تزوجت من السيّدة عطيّات الأبنودي مخرجة الأفلام التسجيليّة.

في عام ١٩٦٦ قبض عليّ مع مجموعة من أصدقائي الكتّاب والشعراء واودعنا المعتقل لمدّة ستة شهور متّهماً بتكوين منظّمة شيوعيّة.

انطلقت أدور القرى والمدن البعيدة ألقي أشعاري في التجمّعات العمّاليّة والفلّاحية والتجمّعات، ولم أجد صعوبة في التواصل مع شعبي بلهجتي الصعيديّة ونوعيّة ما أطرحه من قضايا تهم الشعب.

كان الأضطهاد الدائم هو العقاب المسلّط عليّ لكنّي استطعت أن أكوّن لشعري قاعدة واسعة من الجماهير التي تعرفني جيداً.

MODERN STANDARD ARABIC READING PASSAGE FOR SYRIAN PARTICIPANTS

نشأتُ في حيّ شعبي في دمشق وهو حيّ الميدان لأسرة محافظة. وكان أبي تاجراً فيما مضى، إلّا أنّ الحرب العالميّة الثانية أفلسته تماماً ممّا اضطرّني للعمل صيفاً في معمل الكبريت القريب لأوفّر دراستي شتاء، وذلك عندما كنت في صف الكفاءة.

كنت وأنا طفل شغوفاً بقراءة القصص والروايات، وكنت استأجرها من دكّان قرب الجامع الأموي، وكانت سلسلة "روايات الجيب" هي رائجة آنذاك، وكانت في أعدادها الممتازة تختصر روائع الأدب العالمي. فلم أبلغ الصف الابتدائي الخامس إلّا وكنت قد قرأت معظمها إلى جانب الروايات التاريخيّة الساحرة المترجمة ترجمات كاملة لدوماس الأب والابن، ومترجمات المنفلوطي غير الدقيقة عن الكتاب الرومانتيكيّين الفرنسيّين والألمان، وهذا يبدو غريبا في نظر تلاميذ هذه الأيّام الذين لا يكادون وهم في مثل هذا الصف يفكّون الحرف أو يؤلّفون جملة مفيدة.

وكان أخي عادل يملك مكتبة جيدة من التراث فانكببت عليها أفهم منها ما استطيع واستفهم عما يعسر فهمه، إلى أن أبي كان مغرماً بالسير الشعبية، فقد كان يدعوني وأصدقاؤه لأقرأ لهم سيرة عنترة والزير وتغريبة بني هلال وزاد كل ذلك من حبي لعالم القصّة والرواية المدهش.

قلت إنّ عائلتي كانت محافظة، وكان أبي يرسلني إلى المشايخ مساء وصباحاً قبل دوام المدرسة لأدرس عليهم القصة واللغة العربية، وعايشتهم زمناً ولكنّي كنت أقارن بين حياتهم، مفاهيمهم وعلم قراءاتي الواسع المشرق امطل على أفق المستقبل، فأشعر بشرخ في مفاهيمي، فصرت أتغيّب عن الدروس وعن المدرسة أيضاً

أحياناً وأغرق في المكتبة الظاهريّة، فقرأت هناك على صغر سنّي طه حسين* والعقاد والمازني والحكيم* وغيرهم، وأذكر أن قيم المكتبة تردد في المساح [السماح] لي بالاشتراك وهو ينظر إلي وكأنه يفكر بأنني أتلهى وأهرب من المدرسة وأعبث بالكتب، ولكنه لما رأى إصراري أخذ يتفحصني بعناية، ثمّ فحص ثقافتي وطلب إلي أن أتحدّث إليه عن الكتب التي أستعيرها فأعجب بي، وأخذ يساعدني في انتقاء الكتب، ويدلني على أهمية بعض الفصول. وهكذا اطّلعت على جبران والريحاني ونعيمة* والمهجريين والمصريّين وأنا في صف الكفاءة.

في ذلك الوقت أخذت أقرض الشعر على استيحاء [استحياء] وأكتب بعض القصص من واقع أسرتي وحيّي الشعبي ولكن بلغة قاموسيّة صعبة، وعندما قرأتها لأصدقائي لم يفهموا أكثرها، فكان ذلك درساً لي نبّهني إلى أهميّة البساطة والإفهام والإيصال ممّا ترك أثراً على كتاباتي اللاحقة.

Notes

The author is grateful to professors Kristen Brustad and Barbara Bullock for their input regarding the design and execution of this study. This material is based on work supported by the National Science Foundation Graduate Research Fellowship under Grant No. DGE-111000.

1. My special appreciation goes to Dr. Lama Nassif and Dr. Iman Soliman for their assistance in this regard.
2. α-level = .05
3. p-values for multiple comparisons were determined by Tukey's HSD post hoc test.
4. Pairwise p-values for interactions have been subjected to the Bonferroni adjustment for multiple comparisons.
5. It is important to note that, because of the presence of significant interactions on the basis of allophone for all four speakers' F2 measures, these individuals' results for the variables of quality and dispersion are likely not entirely independent and should not be evaluated as such; however, as each variable is revelatory in its own right, both have been included in the discussion here.
6. The term "diglossic shift" is intended here as a direct counterpart of the more commonly used "style shift" and thus refers to individual instances of change in register marked by alternation between basilectal and acrolectal forms. This differs from the occasional use of the term to refer to community-level changes in the nature of diglossic practices themselves (e.g., Rowe and Grohmann 2013).

References

Albirini, Abdulkafi. 2016. *Modern Arabic Sociolinguistics: Diglossia, Variation, Code-Switching, Attitudes and Identity*. London: Routledge.

Amara, Muhammad, Bernard Spolsky, and Hanna Tushyeh. 1999. "Sociolinguistic Reflexes of Socio-Political Patterns in Bethlehem: Preliminary Studies." In *Language and Society in the Middle East and North Africa: Studies in Variation and Identity*, ed. Yasir Suleiman, 58–80. London: Routledge.

Badawi, El-Said. 1973. *Mustawayāt al-Lughah al-ʿArabiyyah fī Miṣr* [Levels of the Arabic language in Egypt]. Cairo: Dār al-Maʿārif.

Bassiouney, Reem. 2009. *Arabic Sociolinguistics*. Washington, DC: Georgetown University Press.

Bell, Allan. 1984. "Language Style as Audience Design." *Language in Society* 13: 145–204.

Brink, James, Richard Wright, and David B. Pisoni. 1998. *Research on Spoken Language Processing, Progress Report 22: Eliciting Speech Reduction in the Laboratory: Assessment of a New Experimental Method*. Bloomington: Speech Research Laboratory, Indiana University.

Brustad, Kristen. 2017. "Diglossia as Ideology." In *The Politics of Written Language in the Arab World*, ed. Jacob Høigilt and Gunvor Mejdell, 41–67. Leiden: Brill.

Campbell, Robert B. 1996. *Aʿlām al-Adab al-ʿArabī al-Muʿāṣir: Siyar wa Siyar Dhātīyah*. Beirut: Franz Steiner Verlag.

de Jong, Kenneth, and Bushra Adnan Zawaydeh. 2002. "Comparing Stress, Lexical Focus and Segmental Focus: Patterns of Variation in Arabic Vowel Duration." *Journal of Phonetics* 30: 53–75.

Embarki, Mohamed. 2007. "Segmental and Prosodic Aspects of Ksar el Kebir's Neo-urban Variety." In *Arabic in the City: Issues in Dialect Contact and Language Variation*, ed. Catherine Miller, Enam Al-Wer, Dominique Caubet, and Janet Watson, 213–29. London: Routledge.

Ferguson, Charles A. 1959. "Diglossia." *Word* 15: 325–40.

Haeri, Nilofar. 1996. *The Sociolinguistic Market of Cairo: Gender, Class, and Education*. London: Kegan Paul.

Harnsberger, James D., Richard Wright, and David B. Pisoni. 2008. "A New Method for Eliciting Three Styles in the Laboratory." *Speech Commun* 50, no. 4: 323–36.

Hinds, Martin, and El-Said Badawi. 1986. *A Dictionary of Egyptian Arabic: Arabic–English*. Beirut: Librarie du Liban.

Labov, William. 1972. *Sociolinguistic Patterns*. Philadelphia: University of Pennsylvania Press.

Maddieson, Ian. 1985. "Phonetic Cues to Syllabification." In *Phonetic Linguistics: Essays in Honor of Peter Ladefoged*, ed. Victoria Fromkin, 203–21. San Diego: Academic Press.

Mejdell, Gunvor. 2006. *Mixed Styles in Spoken Arabic in Egypt*. Leiden: Brill.

Parkinson, Dilworth. 1993. "Knowing Standard Arabic: Testing Egyptians' MSA Abilities." In *Perspectives on Arabic Linguistics V*, ed. Mushira Eid and Clive Holes, 47–73. Amsterdam: John Benjamins.

Rowe, Charley, and Kleanthes K. Grohmann. 2013. "Discrete Bilectalism: Towards Co-overt Prestige and Diglossic Shift in Cyprus." *International Journal of the Sociology of Language* 224: 119–42.

Schilling-Estes, Natalie. 2002. "Investigating Stylistic Variation." In *The Handbook of Language Variation and Change*, ed. J. K. Chambers, Peter Trudgill, and Natalie Schilling-Estes, 375–401. Malden, MA: Blackwell.

Schmidt, Richard W. 1974. "Sociostylistic Variation in Spoken Egyptian Arabic: A Re-examination of the Concept of Diglossia." PhD dissertation, Brown University.

Schulz, David E. 1981. "Diglossia and Variation in Formal Spoken Arabic in Egypt." PhD dissertation, University of Wisconsin-Madison.

Stowasser, Karl, and Moukhtar Ani. 2004. *A Dictionary of Syrian Arabic: English–Arabic*. Washington, DC: Georgetown University Press.

Suleiman, Saleh M. 1985. *Jordanian Arabic between Diglossia and Bilingualism: Linguistic Analysis*. Amsterdam: John Benjamins.

Thomas, Erik A. 2011. *Sociophonetics: An Introduction*. Basingstoke, UK: Palgrave Macmillan.

Trudgill, Peter. 1986. *Dialects in Contact*. Oxford: Basil Blackwell.

Versteegh, Kees. 2014. *The Arabic Language*. Edinburgh: Edinburgh University Press.

Walters, Keith. 1996. "Diglossia, Linguistic Variation, and Language Change in Arabic." In *Perspectives on Arabic Linguistics VIII*, ed. Mushira Eid, 157–200. Amsterdam: John Benjamins.

Warner, Natasha. 2012. "Methods for Studying Spontaneous Speech." In *The Oxford Handbook of Laboratory Phonology*, ed. Abigail C. Cohn, Cécile Fougeron, and Marie K. Huffman, 621–33. Oxford: Oxford University Press.

Wehr, Hans, and J. Milton Cowan. 1994. *A Dictionary of Modern Written Arabic (Arabic–English)*, 4th ed. Urbana, IL: Spoken Language Services.

Part, Whole, and a Grammaticalization Path for *ši* + NP

■

Peter Glanville, University of Maryland, College Park

This article argues that the semantic constant shared by the quantifier, indefinite determiner, and approximator uses of the construction *ši* + NP in a number of Arabic dialects is an underlying part–whole relation. It proposes a grammaticalization path in which these three uses of *ši* + NP are ultimately derived from the partitive construction *šay' min* "something of," beginning with the quantifier and ending with the approximator. The key innovation that allows this development is a reanalysis in which *šay'* ceases to be a head noun with lexical content, functioning instead as a modifier marking a noun as an indefinite instance conceptualized within a larger whole. After this reanalysis, successive uses of *ši* + NP continue to express a part–whole relation but in an increasingly abstract way, being further and further removed from the transparency of the original partitive.

Key words: Arabic, *ši*, grammaticalization, partitive, quantifier, indefinite determiner, approximator, part–whole relationship

Introduction

In several dialects of Arabic, the construction *ši* + NP is used for three different purposes: to express a quantity, to express an indefinite singular entity, or to express an approximate number.

(1) *ši bxuṛ* "some incense"
(Moroccan; Abdel-Massih 1974, 126, in Obler 1975, 65)

ši kəlma qbīḥa "some ugly word"
(Moroccan; Brustad 2000, 19)

ši mīt sini "about one hundred years"
(Lebanese; Fairouz lyric, Wilmsen 2014, 52)

The modifier *ši* in these examples is widely held to be a grammaticalized form of Classical Arabic *šay'* "thing," which is also taken as the lexical source of the negative enclitic *-š* and the polar interrogative marker *ši,* both exemplified in (2).

(2) *mā* *rafa'-t-əš* *'īd-i*
NEG raised-I-NEG hand-my
"I didn't raise my hand."
(Cairene; Brustad 2000, 284)

'am-tə-'ṣod *ši* *'ən-ni* *kazzāb?*
PROG-you-mean INT that-I liar
"Are you implying that I'm a liar?"
(Damascene; Cowell 2005, 378)

Lameen Souag (2016, 228) observes that the development of š-negation has received a great deal of attention in diachronic work on Arabic, almost to the exclusion of the other derivatives of *šay'* "thing." The aim of this article is therefore to propose a path of development for the quantifier, indefinite determiner, and approximator uses of *ši* + NP given in (1), complementing existing scholarship that establishes a grammaticalization path for *ši* as a negator and marker of the polar interrogative. Counter to Werner Diem (2014), I take *ši* + NP to be a reduced form of the partitive *šay' min* "something of," and I argue for a developmental sequence in which the partitive first gives rise to the quantifier use of *ši* + NP. This in turn facilitates the indefinite determiner use and, from there, the approximator. I show that each of these four related uses of *šay'*/*ši* construes a relationship between a single indefinite instance, or part, and an entirety, or whole, consisting of multiple potential instances, all of which are identical. A part–whole relation is therefore a semantic constant linking the partitive and the various uses of *ši* + NP.

I begin by briefly outlining the grammaticalization path proposed by Diem (2014) and Lucas (2007, 2009, 2015) for negator and polar interrogative *ši*, whereby an adverbial use of *šay'* "a bit" is reanalyzed in certain contexts as meaning "at all," with the important point for the proposal to follow being that this reanalysis allows the subsequent spread of *šay'* into other domains of use. I then turn to the path I propose for *ši* + NP, arguing for a reanalysis in which *šay'* loses its status as the head noun of the partitive construction, where it denotes an indefinite instance or "thing" itself, to become the modifier of the head noun in *ši* + NP, now simply marking the following noun as denoting an indefinite instance that is part of a whole. I show how this part–whole relation remains constant in all uses of *ši* + NP, illustrating also that the uses become more abstract and further removed from what the partitive denotes as the grammaticalization path proceeds. I conclude with a discussion of when and where the path may have begun, and point out the centrality of the part–whole relationship to the separate development of negator and polar interrogative *ši* as well.

Grammaticalization and Negator *ši*

Grammaticalization is a process in which a word loses its lexical meaning in some uses, coming to serve a grammatical function instead (see, for example, Bybee 2003; Bybee, Perkins, and Pagliuca 1994; Heine, Claudi, and Hünnemeyer 1991; Heine and Kuteva 2007; Hopper and Traugott 1993; Traugott and Heine 1991; Wischer and Diewald 2002). It is commonly assumed, and in many cases explicitly stated, that grammatical *ši* is derived from a word meaning "thing": *šay'* in Classical Arabic and *šī* or some variant thereof in the modern spoken varieties (Diem 2014; Esseesy 2009, 2010; Lucas 2007, 2010, 2013, 2015; Obler 1975, 1990). A recent challenge to this line of thought comes from David Wilmsen (2014), who proposes that the source of grammatical *ši* is a proto-Semitic presentative particle **ša*, predating Arabic *hā*, evidence for which is provided by Akkadian third-person demonstrative pronouns: *šu*, *ši*. His argument is that this particle gave rise to an existential particle *še* "there is," beginning a chain of developments in which it is reanalyzed as meaning "it is," then "is it," taking on a polar interrogative function, and from here becoming a marker of negation because of its inclusion in negative responses to interrogatives: "not is."

Wilmsen's proposal is categorically rejected by Al-Jallad (2015) primarily because of its incompatibility with historical phonology. He explains that the [š] of the Akkadian pronouns is descended from one of two possible sibilants in proto-Semitic but that neither of these ever developed into [š] in Arabic, which is descended from a third proto-Semitic sibilant. This means that Arabic *ši* cannot possibly share an ancestor with the Akkadian pronouns that Wilmsen claims as evidence of the presentative **ša,* vitiating the basis of his analysis (see also Pat-El 2016). In addition to this, Wilmsen asserts that lexical *šay'* "thing," rather than being the source of *ši,* is also ultimately derived from the existential particle *še* "there is," but Al-Jallad notes that a verb **śayi'a* "to experience want, to lack" is found in Safaitic (cf. Classical Arabic *šaa'a*) and that although a noun of the same root is attested in the Safaitic inscriptions, there are no grammatical function words. This contradicts what Wilmsen's analysis predicts, since if *šay'* is derived from the existential particle, then that particle should also be found in the Safaitic data. Instead, Al-Jallad concludes that the noun meaning "thing" is derived from the verb noted above, and likely once meant "something desired or lacking." This proposal is strengthened by the fact that the noun *ḥaadʒa* "a need," derived from *'iḥtaadʒa* "to need," has also come to mean "thing" in some dialects, most notably Egyptian Arabic and Maltese.

Further detailed critiques of Wilmsen are offered by Lucas (2015) and Souag (2016), but putting his argument aside, the question then becomes how it is that different functions of grammatical *ši* have arisen from a single lexical source. Diem (2014) argues that negative *ši* results from a reanalysis of the accusative *šay'an* "a thing, a bit," which then becomes an emphatic adverb with a meaning similar to "at all," and eventually a general marker of negation. He is careful to point out that this possibility is raised but ultimately not pursued by Christopher Lucas (2009, 2010) and Lucas and Elliot Lash (2010), although it should be noted that Lucas (2015) returns to this analysis with more conviction. Both authors therefore appear to agree that negative *ši* has developed from uses like those in (3), cited by Diem (2014, 15).

(3) *lan* *ya-ḍurr-ū* *l-lāh-a* *šay'-an*
NEG 3-harm-MPL the-God-ACC thing-ACC
"They will not harm God a bit/at all."

(Qur'ān 47:32)

mā *lā* *ya-nafa'-u-kum* *šay'-an*
what NEG 3-benefit-INDIC-you thing-ACC
"That which does not benefit you a bit/at all."

(Qur'ān 21:66)

Diem (2014, 19) notes that this use of *šay'* to emphasize negation is restricted to the modification of verbs that are quantifiable, meaning that the actions they describe can be measured by degree. An action like harming or benefiting can be done to lesser or greater extents, whereas something like killing is absolute and cannot be done only a bit. In this function adverbial *šay'-an* "conveys the concept that the quantity of the action does not amount to more than a bit or, in negative form, to as much as a bit, which means to nothing at all" (Diem 2014, 19). From here, *šay'-an* is reanalyzed as meaning "at all" and generalized to a larger number of contexts, eventually becoming a marker of negation, which need not be emphatic, and reducing in form in many cases to the enclitic –*š*.

Lucas (2013, 2015) argues that this grammaticalized adverb also accounts for the appearance of *ši* in polar interrogatives in some dialects, and to a lesser extent in conditional clauses. Having taken on the meaning "at all" through its use as an accusative adverb, *šay'* or one of its reflexes is extended to questions in which it functions as a kind of hedge, making the question less direct, and to conditionals, where it may be paraphrased as "at all," or "by any chance." In many dialects this adverb has become restricted to polar interrogatives, but Lucas (2010, 2015) posits that its use in Maltese is closer to what would have been its original distribution more widely. Note that traditionally -*š* is transcribed as -*x* in Maltese.

(4) *intom-x* *ta-raw* *il-postijiet* *fejn . . . ?*
2PL-š 2PL-see the-places where
"Do you see the places where . . . ?"

jekk *t-rid-x* *żwieġ*
if 2PL-want-š marriage
"If you want a marriage . . ."

(Maltese; Lucas 2015, 91)

Lucas (2015) remains open to the possibility that the derivation of negative *ši* from *šay'* occurred before the latter gave rise to the grammaticalized negative polarity adverb "at all" but concludes that the development diagrammed in (5) is more likely.

(5)

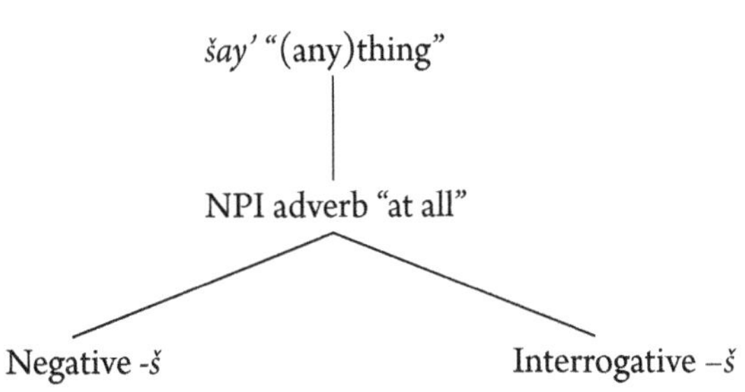

Lucas (2015, 92)

In sum, current scholarship on the derivatives of Classical Arabic *šay'* "thing" favors a grammaticalization path wherein *šay'* is reanalyzed as meaning "at all," and it is this reanalysis that allows it to spread, being used as a negator, a polar interrogative marker, and appearing in conditionals.

A Second Path

The grammaticalization path suggested by Diem and Lucas accounts for the development of negative and polar interrogative *ši* and assumes a second path whereby *ši* + NP develops from the same lexical source, *šay'* "thing," independently of negation. The details of this second path are open for debate, however, and in this article, I argue for the sequence in (6).

(6) Partitive > Quantifier > Determiner > Approximator

Importantly, the shift from a partitive construction to the use of *šay'* as a quantifier is characterized by a change in which *šay'* ceases to be a head noun with at least some lexical content, becoming instead the modifier of the quantified noun. This shift facilitates the subsequent development of the determiner and approximator uses.

Partitive

The source construction from which *ši* + NP is derived is partitive *shay' min* "something/anything of," a construction containing two nouns, in which the first denotes a part found within the referent of the second. The examples in (7) are from the Qur'ān.

(7)	*wa*	*'in*	*fāta-kum*	*šay'-un*	*min*	*'azwāʤ-i-kum*
	and	if	left.3M-you	thing-NOM	from	partners-GEN-your

"And if any of your wives leaves you . . ."

(Qur'ān 60:11)

wa	*la-na-bluw-anna-kum*	*bi-šay'-in*
and	CERTAINTY-we-test-CERTAINTY-you	with-thing-GEN

mina l-xawf-i	*wa*	*l-ʤuw'-i*
from the-fear-Gen	and	the-hunger-Gen

"And we will certainly test you with something of fear and hunger."

(Qur'ān 2:155)

wa	*šay'-in*	*min*	*sidr-in*	*qalīl-in*
and	thing-GEN	from	lote tree.COLLECTIVE-GEN	little-GEN

". . . and a few lote trees"

(Qur'ān 34:16)

It is important to note that the referent of the second noun in the partitive construction is unique, regardless of whether it is marked as definite. The plural noun *'azwādʒ-i-kum* "your wives" refers to a specific set of wives, while *al-xawf* "fear" and the collective noun *sidr* "lote trees" denote certain types or kinds of things rather than particular individual instances (cf. Carlson 1977; Fassi Fehri 2004). A kind (of emotion, of tree) may be thought of as a master category or genus, which although it may be instantiated by specific instances is itself unique because it is different to every other kind. In combination with these nouns in the partitive construction, *šay'* consistently functions to denote part of whatever the second noun refers to: any wife from the set denoted by *'azwādʒ-i-kum* "your wives," an instance of fear rather than fear as a general concept, and a set of lote trees rather than the genus. Two further examples, (8) and (9), from *One Thousand and One Nights* cement the point.

(8)

dʒā'-ū	*'ilay-ya*	*bi-šay'*	*min*	*aṭ-ṭa'ām*
came-3MPL	to-me	with-thing	from	the-food

"They brought me a bit of/some food."

(BYU Corpus: 1001N468:2)

fī	*xāṭir-ī*	*šay'*	*min*	*al-laḥm*	*al-mašwī*
in	mind-my	thing	from	the-meat	the-grilled

"I have a bit of/some grilled meat in mind."

(BYU Corpus: 1001N59:9)

The second noun in these partitives refers to a general concept: food or grilled meat, but it could equally refer to a specific definite instance depending on the context. Hence, *šay' min aṭ-ṭa'ām* "a bit of/some food" can be extended to *šay' min aṭ-ṭa'ām allaḏī ṭabaxtu-hu* "a bit of/some of the food that I cooked." In both cases, however, it remains the case that the referent of the second noun is unique, while the construction as a whole construes an entity that is somehow part of this unique whole and is therefore identical to other potential parts: to other instances of food, of meat, and so on. This is similar to Chung-Ying Cheng's (1973) observation that any part of a mass is identical to that mass, with the difference here being that the identity holds not between the part and the whole but rather between the potential parts of which the whole is composed. Hence, *šay'-un min'azwādʒ-i-kum* can denote a single wife, which is not identical to the whole set of wives but is identical to the other individual wives that compose the set.

When a noun appears as the second noun in the partitive, its referent, the entirety of a class or set, is necessarily conceptualized as divisible since otherwise it would not be possible to isolate only a single instance. The very notion of divisibility means that an entity is not an inviolable whole but rather consists of a potentially indefinite number of identical parts. There are two important clarifications here. First, divisibility is not necessarily a property inherent in the noun itself. The nouns *al-xawf* "fear" and *al-laḥm* "meat" do not refer to collectivities consisting of discrete components. Rather, it is the placement of the noun in the partitive construction that imposes the notion of divisibility on it. Hence, in the partitive, *al-xawf* "fear" and *al-laḥm* "meat" do become divisible, and this is what makes it possible to highlight an instance of fear or a piece of meat profiled against the whole. Second, divisibility as I refer to it here should not be conflated with the part–whole relation construed by the partitive. The part–whole relation is concerned only with the isolation of one component entity from its larger host or class, whereas divisibility is an abstraction imposed on that class. If a referent is viewed as divisible, it can be divided potentially indefinitely into identical elements. Thus, while *šay' min al-xawf* "something of fear" and *šay' min al-laḥm* "a bit of/some meat" divide one instance of fear or meat from the whole, the fact that this is possible means that this whole can be divided over and over. The second noun in the partitive therefore always refers to a divisible entity consisting of potential elements, and the partitive expresses the division of one of these potential elements from the entirety of all the others. I represent the partitive construction pictorially in (9).

(9)

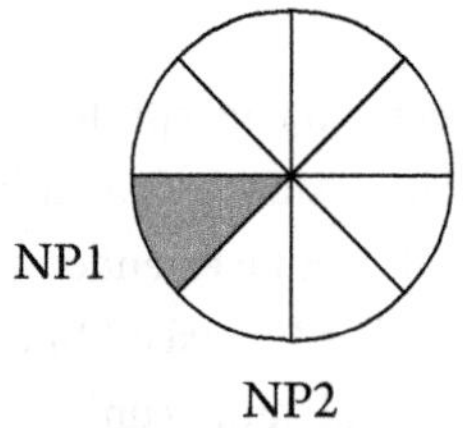

The divided circle in the diagram represents the entirety of all potential instances that compose a whole class or set, and each potential instance is a segment of the circle. Note that this applies even when the whole is a mass like meat, since in the partitive it is conceptualized as divisible and parts of it can be extracted. This whole or entirety is denoted by the second noun in the partitive, NP2. The gray segment is an indefinite instance of the entirety denoted by *šay'*, NP1 in the partitive. I show in the coming sections that this part–whole relationship remains constant in the three uses of *ši* + NP presented in (1).

Quantifier

Three uses of grammatical *ši* are sometimes lumped together under the label of indefinite determiner, but since there is a difference in meaning it is useful to maintain a separation of terminology as well. With collective, plural, and mass nouns, *ši* is best described as a quantifier. Contemporary examples are given in (10).

(10) *šī* *laḥme*
some meat
"Some meat"
(Damascene; Cowell 2005, 467)

səlləf-ni *ši* *flūs*
lend.IMPER-me some money
"Lend me some money"
(Moroccan; Harrell 2004, 69)

'and-u *mimma* *gamī'-u* *'iši gibna* *w* *'iši zatūn* *w*
at-him of-what all-it some cheese and some olives and
'iši *sardīn*
some sardines
"He has a bit of everything: some cheese, some olives, some sardines..."
(Cairene; Badawi and Hinds 1986, 25)

Like the partitive, this use of *ši* + NP construes an indefinite instance of a unique entity—in this case, a quantity of that entity. The difference lies in the grammatical function of *ši* in the two constructions and its relationship to the following noun. Specifically, *ši* has changed from being the head noun in the partitive construction to being the modifier of a head noun in the quantifier construction (cf. Davies 1981, 273). Elizabeth Traugott (2008) shows that this type of change is characteristic of the historical development of English degree modifiers such as *sort of* and *a lot of*. She observes that in an initial "NP1 of NP2" construction, exemplified by *a (special) sort of a rose*, NP1 is the head since the phrase is ultimately about the sort or type and its category membership. This contrasts with examples in which NP2 is the head, such as

(a) sort of a frog, in which *sort* is now a modifier commenting on the extent to which NP2 is like a frog. A similar example would be the contrast between *a bit of a machine,* in which *bit* is the head noun or focus of the phrase, and *a bit of a coward,* in which the construction is no longer partitive and instead *bit of* modifies the head noun *a coward.* Traugott represents this historical shift in which the relationship between NP1 and NP2 undergoes a rebracketing as shown in (11).

(11)	[NP1 [of NP2]]	>	[[NP1 of] NP2]
	Head = NP1	>	Head = NP2
	NP1 + Mod	>	Mod + NP2

(Traugott 2008, 227)

The shift from partitive *šay' min* + NP to quantifier *ši* + NP bears a strong similarity to this observed historical change in English. In the partitive construction, *šay'* denotes an indefinite instance, a "thing," with the remainder of the construction providing the divisible entirety of which that thing is a member. In many contexts this ultimately results in the expression of a quantity of NP2, as with *šay' min al-laḥm* "some(thing of) meat," for example, and it is not difficult to imagine a reanalysis in which *šay'* is viewed as a modifier of the quantified noun. This shift is diagrammed in (12).

(12)

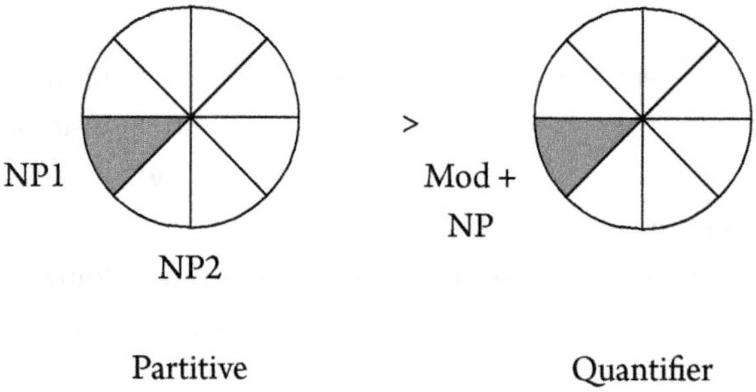

It is important to note that the underlying relationship between a part and a divisible whole does not change here. The difference lies only in how that relationship is expressed. In the partitive, NP2 names the entirety or whole that contains NP1. In the quantifier construction, *šay'* has shifted function, becoming a modifier of the head noun. This entire modifier + noun combination now construes an indefinite instance, and there is no separate noun naming the entirety, which is nevertheless present conceptually. Thus, *šī laḥme* names an indefinite instance or quantity of meat, the gray segment in the diagram in (12), and there is no definite noun referring to the entire class comprising all possible instances. The instance is presented while the entirety remains implicit.

Determiner

When it modifies singular nouns, *ši* is an indefinite determiner.

(13) *ka-y-bqa* *ka-y-qūl* *ši* *kəlma qbīḥa*
INDIC-3-keep INDIC-3-say some word ugly
"He keeps saying some bad word."
(Moroccan; Brustad 2000, 19)

lāzim *ni-ʿmil-l-u* *ši* *muqaddime*
must 1PL-do-for-him some introduction
"We must give him some sort of preparation."
(Damascene; Brustad 2000, 20)

bi-t-lā'ī-h *fi* *ši* *fundu'*
INDIC-you-find-him in some hotel
"You'll find him in some hotel"

ʿand-ak *ḥassāsiyya* *mi* *ši* *dawa*
at-you allergy from some medicine
"Do you have an allergy to any medicine?"
(Levantine; Wilmsen 2014, 53)

Kristen Brustad (2000, 26, 363) terms this type of *ši* an indefinite-specific article that indicates the partial specification or individuation of a given referent in the mind of the speaker. It should be pointed out here, though, that this does not necessarily imply that the speaker knows the exact identity of the referent but rather only that a unique entity exists, known or unknown, somewhere "out there." In (13) the speaker does not seem to be aware of the exact hotel or the exact medicine in question, for example. It is useful at this point to consider the meaning contrast between indefinite determiner *ši* and the zero article. Compare the third example in (13) with (14).

(14) *bi-t-lā'ī-h* *fi* *fundu'*
INDIC-you-find-him in hotel
"You'll find him in a hotel."

In each example the noun *fundu'* "hotel" is indefinite, and neither example seems to suggest more specificity than the other in the mind of the speaker. They differ, however, in that *ši fundu'* brings with it the implication that the speaker wishes to construe the identity of the hotel as unimportant, while *fundu'* alone is neutral. Following Sam Warfel (1972) and Catherine Mazodier (1998), Michael Israel (1999) observes that English *some* in sentences like *there's some guy here to see you* "suggests that for whatever reason the speaker either cannot or will not specify the identity of the referent" (Israel 1999: 174). Just as with *ši fundu'* "some hotel," an expression like *some guy* does not only introduce a unique referent but also carries with it the implication that a more specific identity exists but is withheld. Loraine Obler (1975, 66) makes a similar point, considering *ši* a "pointed marker of non-specificity," and translating *ši kitāb* as "some book, any book, I don't care which book." She states that use of *ši* "emphasizes that the speaker is not concerned with any particular item, whether or not he has knowledge of it, but that he refers rather to any member, members, or quantity of the general class his N delimits" (Obler 1975, 66). Obler goes on to suggest that the determiner use of *ši* has grown out of contexts in which a speaker deliberately expressed a lack of specificity, providing first *šay'* "something" and then a second noun to give further information, as in *šay'-un, ḥimār-un* "something, a donkey" (Obler 1975, 115).

Diem (2014, 106) finds this possibility the most plausible explanation for the development of the determiner construction, but it is difficult to imagine the type of expression that Obler suggests recurring with enough regularity that it becomes grammaticalized. An analysis in which the indefinite determiner use of *ši* has arisen independently of the quantifier use is also challenged by the fact that English *some* functions as both a quantifier and a determiner, in *some bread* and *some guy*, respectively, suggesting that quantifier and determiner uses are semantically related. Indeed, the diagram representing the quantifier use of *ši* in (12) works equally well for the determiner. Just as *šī laḥme* "some meat" expresses one instance of meat highlighted against an implicit divisible whole consisting of identical parts, *ši kitāb* "some book" denotes one indefinite book profiled against an entirety consisting of all the books in the world. Each segment of the diagram in (12) is an instance of meat in one case, or a book in the other.

My logic for deriving the determiner from the quantifier, rather than directly from the partitive, is based on similarities between the types of noun that appear in each construction. NP2 of the partitive is typically a mass like *aṭ-ṭaʿām* "food" or a plurality like *'azawaadʒ -kum* "your wives." The head noun of the quantifier construction shares this characteristic. This is not true of the nouns in the determiner construction, which are ungradable, indivisible wholes. In phrases like *ši kəlma qbīḥa* "some ugly word" and *ši fundu'* "some hotel," the referent of the noun cannot be broken down into smaller identical elements. Since the partitive always contains a divisible noun, the reanalysis of *ši* in the partitive as a modifier must have initially resulted in a modifier + divisible noun construction: the quantifier construction, with the determiner construction arising as the result of an extension of this modifier use to nondivisible nouns. That is, speakers came to associate the quantifier construction with the presentation of an indefinite instance highlighted against an implicit entirety and then employed the same construction to present nondivisible nouns as part of an implicit entirety as well. In all uses, this underlying relationship between a part and whole remains constant, but since the determiner use of *ši* does not present a potentially divisible noun, it is further removed from the partitive than the quantifier use.

Diem (2014, 105–6) rejects the analyses of Joshua Blau (1961, 2006) and Humphrey Davies (1981) in which the determiner is diachronically related to the partitive. His reasoning is that, first, NP2 in the partitive is usually marked with the definite article, whereas this is not possible in the determiner construction. Second, the partitive and the determiner serve different functions. Third, there is no reason why *min* "from/of" should have been deleted from the partitive. And fourth, the development of the determiner from the partitive necessitates the argument that *ši* + NP first developed with plural or mass nouns, which is not borne out by historical data. The first three of these objections seem to be rooted in the notion that the development of one use from another should not be accompanied by any change in linguistic form or function. Diem's own work on the development of š-negation illustrates that form and function do change together, however, and it is not clear why the same should not be possible elsewhere in the language. The definite article and *min* are present in the partitive construction to enable reference to something indefinite (NP1) that is part of a unique and therefore definite entity (NP2). The deletion of the definite article and *min* allows this to be achieved more efficiently, using less linguistic material. It produces a construction in which *šay'/ši* marks the head noun as referring to an indefinite instance of an entirety. Viewed in this light, the fact that some elements of the partitive are not present in the quantifier and determiner constructions does not preclude the possibility that the latter are derived from the former. Rather, it is indicative of a process in which linguistic material is lost in order to facilitate more efficient communication.

Diem's fourth objection is based on premodern data that he asserts are illustrative of the indefinite determiner, which he terms the *šay' kitāb* construction. Examples shown are from Diem (2014, 102–3), but note that the transcription is mine and is an approximation only.

(15) *baqā* *ši* *mašaqqa*
remained.3MSG some difficulty
"... there remains some difficulty..."
(1148 CE, letter in Judeo-Arabic sent from North Africa; Toledano 1927, 451; and Hirschberg 1960)

fī *ši* *hadayān*
in (it) some craziness
"There is some craziness to it."
(twelfth century CE, letter in Judeo-Arabic sent from Alexandria; Goitein 1959; and Blau 2006, 357b)

'iḏa *lāḥ* *la-k* *ši* *zahra*
If appeared to-you some flower
"If some flower appears to you."
(The Andalusian poet aš-Šuštarī [d. 1269 CE]: ed. an-Naššār 1960, 103, 13)

Because there are no instances of *šay'* with a plural or mass noun in this early data, Diem concludes that the determiner construction is unlikely to have developed from the partitive by way of a quantifier. If it had, there would most likely be examples of quantifiers in the data as well. However, while it is true that there are only singular nouns here, I would argue that some of these constructions do convey quantities. In particular, *ši mašaqqa* "some difficulty, hardship" and *ši haddayān* "some craziness, incoherent babbling" seem to me to be instances of gradable, divisible entities: "a degree of difficulty" and "an element of craziness," respectively. This is in contrast to *ši zahra* "some flower" and other examples Diem provides, in which the head noun is not measurable or gradable in the same way. Thus, I believe that Diem's data does show the concurrent existence of both the quantifier construction, closer to the partitive in that its head noun is divisible, and the determiner construction, further removed since its head noun is an indivisible whole.

Approximator

A further development past the indefinite determiner construction sees the modifier *ši* taking on the function of an approximator, blurring the precision of the head noun in the same way as English *some* in phrases such as *some one hundred people*. Examples are provided in (16).

(16) *ṣār* *l-i* *ši* *mīt* *sini*
became for-me some hundred years PROG-I.compose
ʿamm-ʾallif *ʿanāwīn* *miš* *maʿrūfi la-mīn*
addresses NEG known for-who
"It's been some hundred years that I've been sending letters to addresses I don't recognize."
(Lebanese; A Fairouz lyric, Wilmsen 2014, 52)

kun-na *hunāk* *ši* *tlāt* *ʾarbāʕ tiyyām*
was-1PL there some three four days
"We were there (about, some) three or four days."
(Palestinian; Obler 1975, 61)

ši *xmsṭāšr kīlu*
about fifteen kilo
"About fifteen kilos"
(Moroccan; Abdel-Massih 1974, 130, in Obler 1975, 65)

Traugott (2008, 228–29) observes a similar development for English *a sort of*, suggesting that its use in certain taxonomic expressions led to an inference that class membership is not exact. The phrase was then reanalyzed as a degree modifier in phrases such as *a sort of a Gentleman*, used to indicate that the referent of the phrase "is not an adequate or prototypical exemplar of NP2" (Traugott 2008, 229). I suggest that along the same lines, the fact that the indefinite determiner construction exemplified by *ši kitāb* "some book" presents the head noun as unidentifiable within its class has led to an association between that construction and vagueness or underspecification, allowing its extension to express proximity rather than precision.

More formally, the vagueness or underspecification of the approximator use of *ši* is achieved, I argue, by framing the head noun in a part–whole relationship. Brugman (1984) points out that in one use of English *very*, the adjective modifies a noun that denotes an absolute boundary or extent of a region, as in *she is at the very pinnacle of her career*. Here, *very* signals that the noun *pinnacle*, which already refers to a highest point, is being used in its strictest sense. In a related use, however, exemplified by *the very mountains tremble when the Gods become angry*, the noun itself does not denote an extent. Rather, the use of *very* imposes this interpretation on the noun. In this example, Brugman asserts that the use of *very* implies that the mountains and everything smaller tremble because of the Gods. Hence, *very* does not work to accentuate some inherent semantic feature of the mountains but is used here to "impose, rather than evoke, the structure of an extent" (Brugman 1984, 22). In a similar way, the approximator construction imposes a part–whole relationship on the head noun, presenting it as one part of an implicit entirety. For example, the phrase *mīt sini* "one hundred years," denotes a precise quantity that has no identical brethren with which it composes a whole. In contrast, *ši mīt sini* "some one hundred years" in (16) can be taken to denote any quantity of years falling within some undefined parameters between which multiple quantities are possible, and so it is part of a plurality. The phrase eliminates the absoluteness of one hundred, replacing it with a multitude of acceptable versions of what one hundred is, hence the flexibility in how one hundred can be interpreted. There is an implicit entirety consisting of identical parts here, each a possible version or interpretation of one hundred. The phrase *ši mīt sini* "some one hundred years" thus denotes one indefinite version of one hundred while also construing the fact that other versions exist.

Conclusion

My argument for the grammaticalization path outlined above is based primarily on the semantics of each structure and the level of abstraction compared to the partitive, which leaves the question of where and when these linguistic innovations took place and how they spread unanswered. With regard to š-negation, Diem (2014, 6) finds Cairene Arabic to be the most probable candidate for a starting point (see also Lucas 2007), with the innovation spreading along trade and sea routes. One reason for this line of thinking is that š-negation in Egyptian Arabic is obligatory in most situations, whereas other dialects such as Moroccan, while employing š-negation, also preserve non-š-negation in a number of syntactic structures. The conclusion is that š-negation in Moroccan Arabic has not yet reached the level of generalization found in Egyptian and so is more likely to have been in Egyptian Arabic for a longer period of time (Diem 2014, 6, 76).

For the derivatives of partitive *šay' min*, this situation does not hold since use of *ši* + NP is extremely limited in Egyptian Arabic. Davies (1981, 275) gives some seventeenth-century examples in which *ši* is used as a quantifier. The transcription in (17) is mine.

(17)	*ṭabax-tī*	*l-i*	*ši*	*basilla*	*'aw*	*'adas . . . ?*
	cooked-you	for-me	any	peas	or	lentils

"Did you cook me any peas or lentils?"

mā	*fī-h*	*ši*	*rūḥ*
not	in-him	any	spirit

"There is not any spirit in him."

(seventeenth-century Egyptian; Davies 1981, 275)

Davies notes that this use is restricted to negative statements and interrogatives, in which *ši* functions to emphasize a sense of absoluteness: any quantity of peas (at all), any spirit (at all), and so on, but he also points out that modern-day *'iši* in phrases such as *'iši zatūn* "some (quantity of) olives" is an indefinite quantifier used outside of the restricted contexts for which he has data. Based on this, it seems reasonable to conclude that the reanalysis of the partitive in which *ši* becomes a modifier did take place in some limited contexts in Egyptian Arabic, but that this reanalysis did not lead to the indefinite determiner and approximator uses. In contrast, there is evidence that the reanalysis of the partitive had taken place in Morocco and Andalusia by 1148–1300 CE (Diem 2014, 102–3), and Diem's data illustrate both the quantifier and determiner constructions. Grammaticalization has progressed to the approximator function in modern-day Morocco and the Levant, and Obler (1975, 62) notes that *ši* is what she terms an indefinite particle along the Mediterranean coast, Malta but not Cyprus, and in Yemen.

It is therefore unlikely that grammaticalization of the partitive began in Egypt and then spread, but in a model in which linguistic features are spread through interaction of populations it is not clear how the determiner and approximator uses of *ši* could be found on either side of Egypt, apparently having skipped that country itself. One possibility is that Moroccans visiting Jerusalem spread these innovations to the Levant, but perhaps more likely is that progression from the partitive to the approximator function in both regions occurred spontaneously rather than having spread from one location to another. Obler (1975, 116–17) suggests that while the distribution of š-negation in Arabic dialects does appear to result from geographical spread, the instances of indefinite article *ši* in Moroccan and Palestinian Arabic have no obvious historical connection, perhaps having developed in parallel because of some "dynamic internal to a language family" Obler (1975, 116).

The analysis that I have presented here allows for spontaneous developments since it provides a semantic connection between the partitive and the different uses of *ši* + NP that could motivate the same innovations in separate locations. The path I have proposed is supported by the historical development of degree modifiers in English and is in line with general principles of grammaticalization, in which the meaning attributed to a construction becomes more abstract and therefore more removed from the meaning of the source construction over time. It is also interesting to note that, while I maintain that the development of *ši* + NP on the one hand and *ši* in negation and interrogatives on the other are entirely separate, the same part–whole relationship is central to both. Just as the three uses of *ši* + NP that I have outlined above all construe an instance highlighted against an entirety, Diem's source of negator *ši*, accusative *šay'* "a bit/at all," also denotes one instance within an entirety of possibilities. In examples such as *lā yanafa'u-kum šay'-an* "it does not benefit you a bit/at all," the action of the verb is presented as gradable or quantifiable (Diem 2014, 12, 19), and *šay'* denotes one instance or one degree of this gradable entity. The part–whole, or instance–entirety relationship is therefore central to both of the grammaticalization paths taken by *šay'* and is certainly central, more generally, to how we as humans process the events and objects around us.

References

Abdel-Massih, Ernest. 1974. *Advanced Moroccan Arabic*. Ann Arbor, MI: Center for Near Eastern and North African Studies.

Al-Jallad, Ahmad. 2015. "What's a Caron between Friends? A Review Article of Wilmsen (2014), with Special Focus on the Etymology of Modern Arabic ŠI." *Bibliotheca Orientalis* 72, no. 1–2: 34–46.

aš-Šuštarī. N.d. *Dīwān Abī l-Ḥasan aš-Šuštarī*. Ed. 'Alī Sāmī an-Naššār. Alexandria, 1960.

Badawi, Elsaid, and Martin Hinds. 1986. *A Dictionary of Egyptian Arabic*. Beirut: Librairie du Liban.

Blau, Joshua. 1961. *A Grammar of Mediaeval Judeo-Arabic*. [Hebr.]. Jerusalem: The Hebrew University Magnes Press.

———. 2006. *A Dictionary of Mediaeval Judeo-Arabic Texts*. [Hebr.] Jerusalem: Israel Academy of Sciences and Humanities.

Brugman, Claudia. 1984. "The Very Idea: A Case Study in Polysemy and Cross-Lexical Generalization." In *Chicago Linguistic Society Papers from the Parasession on Lexical Semantics*, ed. David Testen, Veena Mishra, and Joseph Drogo, 21–38. Chicago: Chicago Linguistic Society.

Brustad, Kristen. 2000. *The Syntax of Spoken Arabic: A Comparative Study of Moroccan, Egyptian, Syrian and Kuwaiti Dialects*. Washington, DC: Georgetown University Press.

Bybee, Joan. 2003. "Cognitive Processes in Grammaticalization." In *The New Psychology of Language*, ed. Michael Tomasello, 145–68. Mahwah, NJ: Erlbaum.

Bybee, Joan, Revere Perkins, and William Pagliuca. 1994. *The Evolution of Grammar: Tense, Aspect, and Modality in the Languages of the World*. Chicago: University of Chicago Press.

BYU Arabic Corpus: http://arabicorpus.byu.edu/.

Carlson, Gregory. 1977. "Reference to Kinds in English." PhD dissertation, University of Massachusetts at Amherst.

Cheng, Chung-Ying. 1973. "Comments on Moravcsik's Paper." In *Approaches to Natural Language*, ed. K. J. J. Hintikka, J. M. E. Moravcsik, and P. Suppes, 286–88. Dordrecht: D. Reidel.

Cowell, Mark W. 2005. *A Reference Grammar of Syrian Arabic: Based on the Dialect of Damascus*. 1964. Reprint, Washington, DC: Georgetown University Press.

Davies, Humphrey Taman. 1981. "Seventeenth-Century Egyptian Arabic: A Profile of the Colloquial Material in Yūsuf Al- Širbīnī's 'Hazz Al-Quḥūf fi Šarh Qaṣīd Abī Šadūf.'" PhD dissertation, University of California, Berkeley.

Diem, Werner. 2014. *Negation in Arabic: A Study in Linguistic History*. Wiesbaden: Harrassowitz.

Esseesy, Mohssen. 2009. "Reanalysis." In *Encyclopedia of Arabic Language and Linguistics*, vol. 4, ed. Kees Versteegh, Mushira Eid, Alaa Elgibali, Manfred Woidich, and Andrzej Zaborski, 37–43. Leiden: Brill.

———. 2010. *Grammaticalization of Arabic Prepositions and Subordinators: A Corpus-Based Study*. Leiden: Brill.

Fassi Fehri, Abdelkader. 2004. "Nominal Classes, Reference and Functional Parameters, with Particular Reference to Arabic." *Linguistic Variation Yearbook* 4: 41–108.

Goitein, Shelomo Dov. 1959. "Letters about R. Yehuda Hallewi's Stay in Alexandria and the Collection of His Poems." [Hebr.]. *Tarbiz* 28: 343–61.

Harrell, Richard. 2004. *A Dictionary of Moroccan Arabic*. 1966. Reprint, Washington, DC: Georgetown University Press.

Heine, Bernd, Ulrike Claudi, and Friederike Hünnemeyer. 1991. *Grammaticalization: A Conceptual Framework*. Chicago: Chicago University Press.

Heine, Bernd, and Tania Kuteva. 2007. *The Genesis of Grammar*. Oxford: Oxford University Press.

Hirschberg, H. Z. 1960. "The Almohade Persecutions and the India Trade: A Letter from the Year 1148." [Hebr.]. In *Y. F. Baer Jubilee Volume*, ed. S. W. Baron, 134–53. Jerusalem.

Hopper, Paul J., and Elizabeth Closs Traugott. 1993. *Grammaticalization*. Cambridge: Cambridge University Press.

Israel, Michael. 1999. "*Some* and the Pragmatics of Indefinite Construal." *Proceedings of the Berkeley Linguistics Society* 25: 169–82.

Lucas, Christopher. 2007. "Jespersen's Cycle in Arabic and Berber." *Transactions of the Philological Society* 105, no. 3: 398–431.

———. 2009. "The Development of Negation in Arabic and Afro-Asiatic." PhD dissertation, Cambridge University.

———. 2010. "Negative -š in Palestinian (and Cairene) Arabic." *Brill's Annual of Afroasiatic Languages and Linguistics* 2, no. 1: 165–201.

———. 2013. "Negation in the History of Arabic and Afro-Asiatic." In *The History of Negation in the Languages of Europe and the Mediterranean*, Vol. 1, *Case Studies*, ed. David Willis, Christopher Lucas, and Anne Breitbarth, 399–452. Oxford: Oxford University Press.

———. 2015. "On Wilmsen on the Development of Postverbal Negation in Dialectal Arabic." *SOAS Working Papers in Linguistics* 17: 77–95.

Lucas, Christopher, and Elliot Lash. 2010. "Contact as Catalyst: The Case for Coptic Influence in the Development of Arabic Negation." *Journal of Linguistics* 46: 379–413.

Mazodier, Catherine. 1998. "'I must have read it in some article': Instabilité Qualitative de *Some* + Discontinu Singulier." *Cahiers de Recherche en Grammaire Anglaise*. Tome 7: 111–26. Ophrys.

Obler, Loraine. 1975. "Reflexes of Classical Arabic šay'un 'Thing' in the Dialects: A Study in Patterns of Language Change." PhD dissertation, University of Michigan.

———. 1990. "Reflexes of Classical Arabic *šay'un* 'Thing' in the Modern Dialects: Synthetic Forms in Language Change." In *Studies in Near Eastern Culture and History*, ed. James Belamy, 132–52. Ann Arbor: Center for Near Eastern and North African Studies, University of Michigan.

Pat-El, Na'ama. 2016. "Book Review of Wilmsen 2014." *Journal of Semitic Studies* 61, no. 1: 292–95.

Souag, Lameen. 2016. "Book Review of Diem 2014 and Wilmsen 2014." *Linguistics* 54, no. 1: 223–29.

Toledano, Jacob Moses. 1927. "Documents from Manuscripts." [Hebr.]. *Hebrew Union College Annual* 4: 449–67.

Traugott, Elizabeth C. 2008. "Grammaticalization, Constructions and the Incremental Development of Language: Suggestions from the Development of Degree Modifiers in English." In *Variation, Selection, Development: Probing the Evolutionary Model of Language Change*, ed. Regine Eckardt, Gerhard Jäger, and Tonjes Veenstra, 219–50. Berlin: Mouton de Gruyter.

Traugott, Elizabeth C., and Bernd Heine, eds. 1991. *Approaches to Grammaticalization*, Vol. 1, *Focus on Theoretical and Methodological Issues*. Amsterdam: John Benjamins.

Warfel, Sam L. 1972. "*Some*, Reference, and Description." In *Mid-America Linguistics Conference Papers*, 41–49. Oklahoma State University, October 13–14.

Wilmsen, David. 2014. *Arabic Indefinites, Interrogatives, and Negators: A Linguistic History of Western Dialects*. Oxford: Oxford University Press.

Wischer, Ilse, and Gabriele Diewald, eds. 2002. *New Reflections on Grammaticalization*. Amsterdam: John Benjamins.

"I slew my love with my own hand"

ON TOLSTOY'S INFLUENCE ON MIKHAIL NAIMY AND THE SIMILARITY BETWEEN THEIR MORAL CONCERNS

■

Maria L. Swanson, US Naval Academy

Mikhail Naimy, one of the creators of the modern Arabic literary tradition, was affected by several literary influences, including a Russian one. This article gives an example of Leo Tolstoy's impact on Naimy's *Memoirs of a Vagrant Soul* or *The Pitted Face* (1917), which repeats Tolstoy's contributions with variation. I discuss this in addition to the influence that Tolstoy exerted as a philosopher, social critic, and writer on Naimy. Both authors also had similar underlying, unresolved psychological complexes, which made Naimy particularly interested in Tolstoy's *The Kreutzer Sonata* (1889). This research contributes to scholarship about the history and development of the modern Arabic literary and translation traditions and the process of world literature, and it sheds light on Arab-Russian cultural ties. It might be used for reading the two novels from a comparative perspective, which follows the modern movement to contextualize literature within different transnational and global movements.

Key words: impact, comparative literature, Russian literature, modern Arabic literature tradition, Tolstoy's influence, Mikhail Naimy, Pen Association, translation movement, Arabic Renaissance

At the beginning of the last century the young Lebanese writer Mikhail Naimy,[1] who was studying at the Orthodox seminary in Poltava, Russian Empire (present-day Ukraine), wrote: "I was unable to do anything except to compare our literature and Russian literature. O Lord, what a huge chasm separates us from the West! In what darkest darkness we live! How hard is the husk with which we have covered life, so that [it has even lost] its kernel. How poor are you, my country that even world stars like Tolstoy have not yet burned through the darkness of your night" (Sab 1, 233[2]). Within a couple of decades this then-unknown writer would be recognized as one of the founders of the modern Arabic literary tradition.

Naimy's reasons for paying special attention to Russian culture can be traced back to his interesting and unusual biography. His life is divided into several long periods spent in different parts of the world (the Levant, Ukraine, the United States), where he experienced different cultures that influenced many of his literary works.

His lifelong love of Russia started long before Poltava, at the school in his native village and at the Nazareth Teacher's College, which had been founded by the Russian Imperial Orthodox Palestinian Society. During his stay in Ukraine, he was shocked by the cultural differences that separated it from the Arabic world and by the dramatic Russian social upheavals, as he was living there during a period between the two Russian revolutions (of 1905 and 1917). Due to this situation, many political, social, and cultural issues occupied his mind more deeply and helped him perceive Russian literature not from the vantage point of a curious onlooker or researcher but as someone who formed a part of Russian society, which was immersed in deep crisis.

Naimy's claim about Arabic literature is similar to Mikhail Lermontov's complaint that his native literature was so poor that he could not borrow anything from it (Meyer 2010, 75). If Lermontov's imitation of Pushkin's prose (who, in turn, had imitated Western works) enabled him to bring Russian prose to the level of Western European literature (76), Naimy's willful repeating-with-variation of Russian literature led to his acceptance and creative rethinking of Russian literary works.

This pattern of influence can be explained by Yuri Lotman's theory of interacting cultures from the late 1930s. He wrote that this dialectical process takes place when representatives of one culture view another "through the lens of their own national self-image and create the construct of [another culture] in contrast with [their] own dominant code" (Meyer 2010, 4).

Naimy repeatedly claimed that he first and foremost owed his discovery of literature to Russian writers. He did not conceal the fact that he used their approaches in his own writings and that they had fostered his spiritual growth. Tolstoy's philosophy turned out to be more influential on Naimy's early writings than any other Lebanese, European, or American writer. The writings of the great Russian philosopher had already attracted Naimy's attention when he was a student at the Nazareth Teacher's College. In Poltava, Tolstoy, through his books and articles, became an important model and imagined interlocutor for Naimy, who admired him and called him "a shining torch" (Sab 1, 124). It is also important to consider that during his stay in Russia, Naimy witnessed nonstop debates all over Russia about Tolstoy's worldwide fame and his heresy. Tolstoy was said to lead a life of flamboyance that bordered on madness beginning after his excommunication from the church in 1901.

The theory of literary influence, with its pervasive anxieties and "strong" and "weak" misreadings, as proposed by the American literary critic Harold Bloom (1997, 2011), suggests how this process developed in Naimy's writings.

The young seminarian noted in his Poltava diary that he wanted to copy Russians in everything and compete with them in playing the violin, declaiming poetry, and, certainly, writing (Sab 1, 175). The sixteen-year-old Naimy passionately argues with Tolstoy in his diary with all his youthful enthusiasm. There he noted, after an analysis of Napoleon's and Mikhail Kutuzov's images in *War and Peace,* that he did not agree with the Russian writer concerning several details: "It is ridiculous of me to object to such a great thinker as Tolstoy. . . . I'm sorry, Leo Nikolaevich" (Sab 1, 189).

During the next stage of his life, while living in the United States, and unlike his literary cohorts from al-Rābiṭa al-Qalamiyya (The Pen Association), he retained strong ties with Russia, whose political, social, and cultural realities were reflected especially in his early writings (Ḥāfiẓ 1997, 171).[3] Aida Imangulieva (1975, 1986, 1991, 2009), who has dedicated several studies in either part or in whole to Naimy, claims that the members of the Pen Association, who proved themselves to be the pioneers of the new Arabic literature, raised it to a new level by diversifying its themes and genres, created new forms of artistic expression, and incorporated foreign literary currents into it largely under the influence of European and American writers. But if Ameen Rihani and Kahlil Gibran became the exponents of this philosophical and literary current together with European romanticism, then Russian literary criticism and realism turned out to be the stronger influences on Naimy's literary works.

Imangulieva (1975, 1986, 1991, 2009) and Naimy (1985) argue precisely that the Russian influences, Tolstoy important among them, laid the groundwork for the Pen Association members to absorb American transcendentalist writings.

We believe that the young and emotional Naimy, who was shocked by the richness and beauty of Russian literature and culture, found in it what he needed. However, he also felt pervasive anxiety toward Russian authors, and he started not just to imitate but to compete with them.

In this article I focus on Naimy's *Memoirs of a Vagrant Soul* or *The Pitted Face* (1917) (hereinafter, *The Pitted Face*), which immediately after its first publication drew the attention of readers and literary critics (Sab 2, 356–57) as an outstanding literary work and an example of how Naimy contributed to the development of the literary hero and novel genre in Arabic literature.

But here we study this novel from a different perspective. We argue that Naimy creatively based the premise of *The Pitted Face* on Tolstoy's *The Kreutzer Sonata* (1889) (hereinafter *KS*). We also attempt to explain why Naimy, who was intolerant of any kind of violence and murder, was attracted to the bloody plot of *KS*.

Tolstoy certainly did not invent "the wife-killing" genre. At the turn of the twentieth century, Eros had started to prevail over Logos in Western European and later Russian literature. The topics of sexual relationships and the woman's role in the family and society became common in literary works, especially in France (Alexandre Dumas, fils, Guy de Maupassant, Émile Zola), and Western European philosophers and psychologists (Sigmund Freud, Arthur Schopenhauer) devoted volumes of their studies to these issues.

Despite an undisputed French influence, Tolstoy established "the opposition between French values and the ideal in order to arrive at a genuinely Russian synthesis, [and his works were] created out of a deeply national culture, using its language . . . , genres . . . , places . . . and subject matter (a moral-philosophical quest, not sensational entertainment)" (Meyer 2010, 7). He wrote *KS* during a critical historic and cultural period when, on the one hand, all the conflicts of the prerevolutionary era were becoming more intense with each passing year, and, on the other hand, the Silver Age in Russian art and literature was about to begin. Quite often literary works of a whole cohort of Russian writers and philosophers created at that time functioned as manifestos of personal ethical and philosophical beliefs (Voronina 2015, 1–4), and they were broadly discussed both in the press and in private conversations.

As mentioned earlier, Naimy was attracted to Tolstoy's judgments about social injustice and the vices that people are susceptible to as well as the latter's criticism of the hypocrisy of the official clerical institutions that were tasked with responding to the sufferings of the people. All these thoughts were reflected in *KS*, the publication of which provoked loud debates and a strong reaction all over Russian society and which was banned by the tsarist government and censored by the Holy Synod.

KS had already drawn the attention of Salim Qubayn (1904), one of the first graduates of Nazareth Teacher's College, before Naimy became interested in Tolstoy's novel. However, Qubayn's translation of the Russian novel failed to preserve its original idea despite his brilliant knowledge of Russian language. It included didactic passages about marriage, morality, and how children should be raised, which would have met with the approval and the tastes of readers of the Arabic Renaissance (Dolinina 2010, 294). Qubayn's work consisted of a pastiche of Tolstoy's original ideas, correct and misinterpreted, and his own ones. Dolinina (295) believes that *KS* drew Qubayn's attention because it engaged topics that were popular at that time owing to Qasim Amin's books about female emancipation. Qubayn wanted to reaffirm Amin's position through the philosophical and literary work of such a popular international writer as Tolstoy.

From this side, *The Pitted Face* is an example of what was considered to be a translation of foreign literary works during the Arabic Renaissance period. It could be *naql* "moving," "conveying" by putting foreign literary works into Arabic context, or *ta'ariib* "Arabizing" by transferring the idea of a text to another one (Scoville 2015, 224) or by applying both models, as it happened to be Naimy's case.

But how did it happen that Naimy was drawn to *KS* out of all of Tolstoy's many works? I argue that, in addition to sympathizing with Tolstoy's social criticism, the Lebanese writer shared similar deep psychological complexes that were characteristic of Tolstoy. In particular, he was influenced by the great Russian writer's ideas about abstinence since he had unresolved issues about the physical side of love. They overlapped with Tolstoy's concerns, and they enabled the Lebanese author to create a very similar novel both in terms of plot and characters.

This novel's narrative frame is the same as *KS* (a story within a story). A stranger is hired at an Arab café in America. He receives the nickname al-'Arqash "The Pitted Face," as his face bears the scars of smallpox. He is always quiet and silent, just like Vasily Pozdnyshev, the protagonist of *KS* at the beginning of Tolstoy's novel. After al-'Arqash vanishes, his diary is found during an investigation. Its pages, which are full of passionate and unorganized notes touching on a broad range of questions, constitute the main narrative frame of *The Pitted Face*. As for *KS*, its central hero breaks into a conversation, and his nervous and expressive monologue, which also consists of several parts, takes up most of Tolstoy's novel.

The Pitted Face ends with a short announcement in a local newspaper about the murder of a bride in a hotel room and the disappearance of the groom. This unexpected bloody turn and ending of this novel, which comes after pages of extensive philosophical speculation, are similar to the ones of *KS* and can be explained by Naimy's desire to imitate Tolstoy's dualism. The great philosopher Tolstoy came to hate women for making him break his sexual abstinence principle, and his misogyny grew with every single passing year (McLean 2008, 205). This attitude can certainly be felt throughout his literary works as well as in numerous letters.

With every new moral crisis, Tolstoy hated more and more what women fundamentally represented in life as well as their bodies, to say nothing of marriage. This is the real reason why Pozdnyshev's wife is murdered, because she symbolizes all women for Tolstoy.

Tolstoy also hated sex, considering it to be "destructive to human sanctity and a massive intrusion on a person's well-being, . . . [and it also represented a] ruthless obliteration of the sanctity of personhood" (Wasiolek 1986, 154, 156). Many of his works are full of examples of sex as a disgusting deed as well as its destructive and even deadly power (Cruise 2002).

For this analysis, I propose the following parallel: Pozdnyshev is "an alter-ego of Tolstoy" (Voronina 2015, 5) in the same way that al-'Arqash is an alter ego of the Lebanese author, who, while addressing him, says "My constant and trusty companion. . . . None were keen enough to know that the ties between you and me were more powerful than time and more enduring than the earth" (*The Pitted Face* 146, 147).[4]

Tolstoy's Pozdnyshev, naturally, shares his author's position toward the physical side of love:

> I from childhood had prepared myself for [what we call love], . . . [as] it was the noblest and highest occupation in the world. . . . However, in practice it is an ignoble and degrading thing, which it is equally disgusting to talk about and to remember, . . . but people pretend that what is ignoble and the shameful is beautiful and lofty.
>
> . . . I thought [all my acts during the honeymoon] were virtuous, and that to satisfy your desires with your wife is an eminently chaste thing, . . . [but marriage is] nothing other than a license to engage in debauchery. . . . I began my honeymoon hoping for great joys. . . . During this entire time I felt anxious, ashamed, and weary. Soon I began to suffer. . . . I abandoned myself to beastly excesses. I was not only not ashamed of them, but proud of them. (*KS* 119)

Naimy's attitude toward women and sex has a lot in common with Tolstoy's position, although the Lebanese writer, in contrast to the Russian one, never married or had children, and he never wrote long, confrontational tracts about the destructive consequences of the physical side of love.

Most of the Lebanese writer's memoirs about his private life and family date back to his youth. All of his numerous later works were devoted exclusively to political, social, and philosophical issues, though he would also insert asides about why he never married. Naimy claimed that he never wanted to do this owing to his very deliberate lifestyle as well as his devotion to his writings. We do not think that this decision was as simple as he tries to present it to his readers. The phrase "I slew my love with my own hand" from Naimy's Poltava diary, when he decided to break up with Varia, a local girl, as their affair had entered a stage in which he could no longer be chaste, is key to our further discussion of Tolstoy's influence on Naimy and the similarity of their positions.

Naimy's al-'Arqash expresses the same point of view about sexual relationship that Pozdnyshev articulates:

> The complex problems of sex [broaden] from the leaping fire of infatuation to the cold ashes there of; from the ecstasy of marital union to its endless headaches, . . . [they are] an enchantment and a disenchantment, a mouthful of honey and a cupful of gall, a flow and ebb, . . . a benediction and a curse, a hopeful prayer and a morbid blasphemy,—all shunning light and breeding in the dark where lowly passions take on the luster of pure virtue, and where the ashes of those passions appear as gold dust. Hearts budding forth to pleasure are quickly occupied by pain. (*The Pitted Face* 75–76)

What did the Russian and Lebanese hermits propose to do to improve a society that was suffering from spiritual bankruptcy and unbelievable levels of corruption? Since, as Tolstoy pointed out in his story *Tri dnya v derevne*, "evil will be destroyed outside of us as soon as it is destroyed inside of us" (1928, 38:10), we need to direct ourselves to fight it by studying our nature and by constantly and mercilessly working toward our self-perfection.

Tolstoy worked out a system of views, but he developed them to an extreme degree. They were completely different from those held by many other world-renowned poets, writers, and philosophers, but they turned out to be mostly shared by the Lebanese and Russian authors. The Lebanese writer arrived at the same idea espoused by the late Tolstoy that a person must build his life based on the idea of good and exceptional morality (Bilyk 1984, 77). This means that spiritual growth must be given priority over the less significant urges of our flesh and blood. Naimy had already written in his Poltava diary: "Of all of the [misdeeds], I hate promiscuity in all its manifestations most of all" (Sab 1, 209).

But the system of special views created by both writers did not include marriage and love between a man and a woman as its important components. Naimy's al-'Arqash shares Pozdnyshev's skeptical and bitter scorn about these topics: "[A man and a woman fall in love]. Then . . . they are impelled by their love to proceed to the altar of marriage . . . to immolate it and to cremate it there and to be immolated and cremated by it. Marriage is love's crematory. . . . While love draws the lovers heavenward, marriage drags them back to earth. . . . Love is a melting, evaporation, and diffusion; marriage is a freezing over, a cracking, and a splitting" (*The Pitted Face* 71). And Pozdnyshev fierily argues with his fellow travelers:

A Lady: Love . . . is a preference for one man or one woman to the exclusion of all others . . .

Pozdnyshev: A preference for how long? . . .

A Lady: For a long time, for a life time sometimes.

Pozdnyshev: But that [never] happens . . . in life, . . . [where] this preference . . . lasts in rare cases several years, oftener several months, or even weeks, days or hours.

A Lady: But you are talking of physical love. . . . [What about] a love based upon conformity of ideals, on a spiritual affinity?

Pozdnyshev: Yes, I affirm that love, real love, does not consecrate marriage, as we are in the habit of believing, but that, on the contrary, . . . ruins it. . . . You say that marriage is based upon love. . . . But in our day marriage is only a violence and falsehood. . . .

Marriages . . . exist for people who . . . do see in marriage something sacramental, a sacrament that is binding before God . . . but to us they are only hypocrisy and violence. . . . We must not preach debauchery. . . .

People marry in the old fashion, without believing in what they do . . . [they take] upon themselves the obligation to live together all their lives (they themselves do not know why), and from the second month have already a desire to separate, but continue to live together just the same. Then comes that infernal existence. . . .

I cannot remember . . . [the days of my engagement] without shame. What an abomination! (*KS* 103–5, 119)

As it comes from the close reading, al-'Arqash and Pozdnyshev make the same conclusion that celibacy and virginity is a good solution and express close views on love. But their views reveal an interesting contrast, which reflects the position of their authors. Naimy's narrator seems to fear that marriage routinizes love and makes it earthbound. This is his author's fairly conventional repudiation of convention.

As for Tolstoy's narrator, he takes the more radical position that there is no such thing as love at all, that it is just a side effect or optical illusion brought on by lust and the need to perpetuate society. There is no pure love that marriage devalues. Rather, there's only debauchery and the attempt to find excuses and acceptable frameworks for it. Tolstoy affirmed this position in his afterword to the *KS* (1982, 197, 198, 199):

It is necessary for the view . . . to carnal love to change. Men and women ought to be educated . . . on infatuation and the carnal love connected with it . . . is degrading to man. . . .

> It is not good because the attainment of the aim of being united in wedlock or of being outside of wedlock with the object of love . . . is unworthy of man. . . . Carnal love is something peculiarly exalted. . . . The aim . . . of man is to serve humanity, his country, science, or art . . . , [it] is not attained through a union with the object of love in wedlock or outside of wedlock, but that . . . infatuation and union with the object of love . . . , [which] never makes the attainment of the aim which is worthy of man any easier, but always impedes it.

Further analysis brings us to the contradiction that Tolstoy and Naimy faced. If we follow Tolstoy's and Naimy's shared concept to its logical conclusion, not only women but also men must remain virgins, as once people stepped away from a pure lifestyle, they joined the source of moral and physical corruption.

Tolstoy's novel showed all that he was feeling in his old age—a deep regret for his immoral behavior during his youth and for the hypocrisy of making his wife stay almost constantly pregnant while at the same time propagating celibacy. Instead of blaming himself, he constantly accused his wife as well as all women in the world of provoking desires and controlling men through their carnality. Pozdnyshev represents Tolstoy's masochism and hypocrisy, as he hates himself and punishes himself for his desires and at the same time constantly criticizes females for their actions and mostly puts the fault on them. Thus, the Russian writer subconsciously transfers the punishment that he has subjected himself to for his own erotic thoughts and deeds to all women.

The Lebanese author demonstrates the similar contradictive position through al-'Arqash's recognition of a man's weak nature: "Man—the lord of creation. How most absurd the notion! . . . [then] . . . sleep, hunger, sex . . . should be . . . obedient to his will . . . watch yourself against yourself" (*The Pitted Face* 81, 82, 44). But in another note Naimy's protagonist proudly declares: "I am a mind endowed with a body, rather than a body endowed with a mind" (*The Pitted Face* 7).

Pozdnyshev and al-'Arqash do not kill themselves because of their deeds. After recovering from their shock, both of them feel something like sorrow for their victim,[5] as only now they realize that they have killed a human, and have not just got rid of an intolerably provocative body. However, their sorrow is mostly due to their own sufferings they experience from seeing the slaughtered bodies. They express similar reactions:

> *Al-'Arqash:* That gaping wound in her throat is still unhealed. That deep fearful sadness in her large eyes. . . . Her face is like ivory: pale and bloodless. . . .

> What can I do for her. . . . This woman appears to me as the very personification of deep, silent sorrow . . . , and her silence overawes me. (*The Pitted Face* 10–11)
>
> *Pozdnyshev:* only when I saw her in the coffin, . . . when I saw her dead face did I understand all that I had done. . . . She, who had been a moving, living, palpitating being, had now become motionless and cold, and that there was no way of repairing this thing. He who has not lived through that cannot understand it. (*KS* 172)

Both of the protagonists are firmly protected by their authors from any kind of punishment or revenge. Naimy even compliments his hero in the end of the novel through finding his memoirs to be "echoes from that harmonious choir of yearnings which is [his] spirit" (*The Pitted Face* 148).

As for Pozdnyshev, who narcissistically thinks that running after his wife's lover in his stockings several minutes after the murder would look ridiculous, and who looks at his now ugly and slighted wife like an outsider, finally relieving from getting rid of a provoker of his sufferings, he receives Tolstoy's feeling and sympathy. The Russian writer admires his protagonist's willpower and endurance when he says: "There is no need to fear. I know what I am doing. . . . I will not kill myself" (*KS* 169).

Tolstoy's hero forgets about the implications of leaving his five children without a mother, and his position is similar to the contradictory one presented by his author. On the one hand, he claims that a husband and wife need to live like brother and sister, and only the decision to have children is sufficient grounds for their sexual relations. On the other hand, Pozdnyshev does not feel anything for his children, as they "torment [him], and nothing more." These thoughts remind us of al-'Arqash, who considers children to constitute part of "complex problems of sex," which include "the passion for children despite the bitter complaints of the pains and responsibilities they entail" (*The Pitted Face* 75).

The Arab al-'Arqash takes his bride's life for a reason very similar to the one that underlies the Russian Pozdnyshev's murder. In fact, Tolstoy's hero does not kill his wife because of his jealousy. The real reason is his anger at modern society for overstepping the boundaries of beautiful and innocent Platonic love and converting it into an animalistic emotion. He is thus absolutely sure that sooner or later a relationship between his wife and someone else will come about as a result of humanity's corrupted nature. Like his author, he is constantly trying to work out his own confusing and unclear moral concepts, and he criticizes people's vices and the modern society.

Sigmund Freud's theory explains the states of mind of al-'Arqash and Pozdnyshev as ones of physiological impotence, which are quite common in modern society.

It affects those whose libido does not develop completely, when the two attachments, the physical and the emotional, converge into one. The heroes of the two novels cannot respond to the beautiful and delicate desires that their wives provoke in them with anything other than rough physical contact, and this feeling makes them hate sex. In their minds, premarital romantic sensuality, tenderness, mystique, and the desire to share one's life with another person and to love holiness acted to convert sex between husband and wife into a permanent exhausting and stultifying relationship with a prostitute. It served only to spawn uncontrolled passions, split personalities, and a sense of being enslaved (Pomerants 2015).

Daniel Rancour-Laferriere (1998) applies the theories of Klein and Freud to argue that Anna Karenina's suicide was a literary expression of Tolstoy's desire to kill himself or to punish himself for his lust, as he hated himself no less than he hated women. That is why Tolstoy's aggression combined masochistic elements directed at himself with sadistic impulses toward women.

Rancour-Laferriere (1998) also concludes that the great Russian writer experienced a deep Oedipus complex and was jealous of his mother and hated all the other men who were associated with his mother in his mind. This claim is supported by the fact that Tolstoy recalled that his mother had been in love and even engaged to another man before she married Tolstoy's father. Thus, he subconsciously makes his readers (and himself) think that she had enjoyed love and sex with another man who was not his father. It allows Tolstoy to win the competition with his father.

This research helps us understand what Naimy might have not even recognized. In his memoirs he talks about Youssef, his father, as though he were a real loser, and thus the Lebanese writer easily wins the Oedipus complex competition. Youssef, who was absent for seven years trying to earn a living in the United States, is depicted by Naimy as someone who was a stranger to him, who did not have much luck in his life, even in America, which he dreamed so much of. Although hard work in the United States brought Naimy's father more grief and loss than real income, his family was able to build a house that was comparably decent for its village, given the amount of money that Youssef was able to earn. This new house immediately placed Naimy's family into another, much more prestigious social category.

Similar positions taken by the two authors allow us to further analyze the shared features of their attitudes to sexual relationships and their behavior toward women. The rivalry between males, which is usually a result of absence of self-confidence, leads to the same behavior pattern. Naimy evokes similar thoughts as Tolstoy's when the Lebanese writer describes in his memoirs the husbands of the ladies with whom he had affairs. These men are depicted as ugly, sick creatures and real losers who are neither able to make a firm decision nor understand life.[6] According to Naimy, they never make their wives happy, either materially or physically. And they are certainly unloved. Similarly, Naimy showed up in the dark and gloomy lives of his lovers. He gives them hope, only to break their hearts and frustrate their desires to have sex with him. But each time he followed the same relationship pattern, the women would take the initiative. He would resist at first, but eventually he would express interest. The end of the relationship comes each time too soon, when Naimy starts to abhor them for their passions and desires. Then he disappears, or a woman's husband shows up, to Naimy's great relief, as he did not want the actual act of adultery to take place. Then he called off these relationships, leaving these ladies with broken hearts but still with some hopes that the affair might resume.

If we further analyze Naimy's private life from his writings, we notice that he was only involved in love affairs with women who were older than him and who were unhappily married. In his actions, al-'Arqash reveals himself to be very much an autobiographical character. He disappears from the place where he was supposed to lose his chastity, leaving a note with the following text: "I slew my love with my own hand, for it was more than my body could feel and less than my soul hungered after" (*The Pitted Face* 143). This phrase almost repeats another one that was already cited above and that provides a key explanation for al-'Arqash's crime. It comes from Naimy's Poltava diary when he decided to immediately break up with Varia. He experienced a panic attack about how he should overcome the next stage in his love story, which he believed put him in a morally impossible position.

Naimy wrote *The Pitted Face* in 1917, about ten years after the Poltava affair, and he rewrote the work and published it in its full form in 1949, when he was sixty years old. What was it about this work that held Naimy's attention over such a long period of time? The answer does not come only from his explanations in the end of *The Pitted Face*, but it is also in his other writings. Among his early literary works, we do not find anything devoted to a romantic relationship or to love between a man and a woman, which is a typical topic for young poets and writers. His lost verse "Funerals of Love," written at the seminary (Sab 1), is an exception. It is easy to guess about the poem's sad content, based on its title. Was it an author's negative experience or a sad story that shocked him?

It is very hard to expect Naimy to make the same categorical judgments that Tolstoy made about women when the former was barely out of his teens, but Naimy's feeling of discomfort with women as well as his lack of self-confidence and rejection of sex can be read throughout his diary:

> We lay down in the grass, but my female friend does not lie down quietly. And I know why. . . . There is a fierce struggle: "Misha, you are experiencing

> an ordeal. Will you overcome it? . . . You must win. You must prove to yourself that you are stronger than this ordeal. You must preserve your honor. You are responsible for this girl. You can turn her towards a debauched way of life. Or you can turn her towards purity; if she has already lost it."[7] . . . She is just a female body to you, and I hated myself [for my physiological reaction to her kisses]. . . . I resisted and controlled myself as much as I could, and I left this battle as a winner: I saved my virginity. (Sab 1, 194–95)

This quotation illustrates feelings that are quite similar to the ones that the young Tolstoy also experienced. He was taken by his brothers to a brothel, where he lost his virginity when he was less than eighteen years old. After that he locked himself in a bedroom and cried for the entire night. A year later Tolstoy worked out a long list of recommendations about the right lifestyle. They included: "Rule number one: [you must] distance yourself from women. [Rule] number two: eliminate your lust through work" (*Izbrannye dnevniki* 8). There is a similar passage in al-'Arqash's diary: "To constrain the needs of the flesh is a virtue. To constrain the needs of the soul is a sin" (*The Pitted Face* 15).

Approximately a decade and a half after the incident with Varia, Naimy proudly confirms his position with al-'Arqash's words addressed to his Eye: "Never did I kindle the fire of any passion in you with my Eye, . . . the passion of Adam for Eve" (*The Pitted Face* 89). This phrase reflects the Gospel of Matthew (5:28), which Tolstoy quoted many times, and it is supported by Pozdnyshev: "Sexual passion, no matter what form it takes, is a terrible evil that must be fought and not encouraged. The words of the Gospel that the man who looks at a woman with lust in his eyes has already committed adultery with her do not apply to looking at someone else's wife, but specifically and most importantly to looking at one's own wife" (*KS* 122).

Our analysis of the specific nature of Naimy's and Tolstoy's relationships with women allows us to conclude that they were haunted by "the tragedy of the bedroom," about which Maxim Gorky once said: "Man suffers through earthquakes, epidemics and horrors of disease together with all sorts of spiritual torments, but the most agonizing tragedy that he will ever know has been and always will be the tragedy of the bedroom" (Gorky, cited in Ramadan 1993, 62).

By relying on Freudian psychoanalysis, we can interpret Gorky's pronouncement in light of the tendency of men to institute a taboo when they feel any kind of danger. The first intercourse with a woman represents an extreme peril for them. That is why the taboo of virginity as well as the other taboos associated with woman, including menstruation, pregnancy, and childbirth, can have a profound impact on the sexual life of men by causing them to feel psychic (and at times physical) impotence.[8] This can be manifested as a temporary erectile dysfunction that is caused by neuropsychiatric disorders (Ramadan 1993, 62). Al-ʾArqash kills his bride when he realizes that this woman, after becoming his wife, will embody Eve by forcing him to violate his puritanical beliefs and constantly desire her body, driven by "the biggest poison, [which is] people's debauchery" (*KS* 131), "the memory of which is swinish, nasty, and shameful" (*KS* 125).

Max Nordau (1993), a physician and social critic, wrote that Tolstoy was a hyper-emotional psychopath with a pathologically excitable sexual center. The same can also partly be said about Naimy because of his abnormal reactions to women. In fact, the intercourse in Tolstoy's writings is often preceded or followed by uncontrolled hysteria, a panic attack, or death. Vronsky's jaws neurotically shake after his sexual contact with Anna; Pozdnyshev experiences the same thing before killing his wife; and al-ʾArqash demonstrates the same neuropsychiatric nature of his author: "My whole body is like a machine whose screws and springs have been set loose. I have lost control of all my muscles. The hands shake; the teeth click; the heart bounces and flutters . . . ; the lungs are about to blow up" (*The Pitted Face* 10).

There is one more key point that we observe in both literary works: al-ʾArqash and Pozdnyshev both use a dagger to commit their murders. This is a natural choice for Naimy's hero since daggers had been traditional Middle Eastern weapons for centuries (Beikham 2016). But our question is, How could he have found that tool in the hotel room that he brought his beloved bride to? Is it a piece of evidence that he had a premeditated intention to kill her, so this murder was an obsessive idea, like Pozdnyshev's? Or was this killing a spontaneous and neurotic reaction of al-ʾArqash to the situation, when he sharply realized that his mind was hopelessly losing its game to his body? In this case, the presence of a dagger in the hotel room was a random coincidence.

Tolstoy's protagonist slays his wife with a dagger that had been hanging on the wall, though in Russia it would have been more common to hang a pistol, revolver, or a shotgun there. It is possible to explain this fact by the influence by Orientalism on Pozdnyshev, which was extremely popular in the Russian Empire at that period. The vogue for the East can in part be attributed to the numerous wars that the Russian Empire had been fighting in the Caucasus at the time. But we can see from earlier drafts of *KS* that Tolstoy, who had been an avid hunter (during the pre–religious crisis period of his life) and owned rifles, was thinking of using a gun as the murder weapon, but then he changed his mind to make it a dagger.

We further claim that the choice of a dagger in these two plots reveals their authors' similar attitude toward sex. Rancour-Laferriere (1998) hypothesizes that the dagger is a long, pointed object, which in this case is used by a man to penetrate the body of a women. Hence, it can be interpreted as a phallic symbol. Thus, both authors believe that the male member is not just a body part but rather a destructive tool. The real murder that takes place at the end of Tolstoy's novel is the final summation of the numerous misdeeds performed by Pozdnyshev during the years when he had sex with his wife, and he sadly states: "I had killed my wife long before [this actually] happened" (*KS* 126). Al-'Arqash echoes him: "Flesh clinging to flesh is soon made to rot and to disintegrate. And blood setting fire to another blood, only turn in the end into deadly pus" (*The Pitted Face* 76).

Tolstoy and Naimy consider love, joy, and sex to be sources of deep pain that are tantamount to murder: Vronsky kills his beloved horse, and Tolstoy killed Karenina, with whom he was in love. The death from *The Pitted Face* repeats a similar theme: "I do not make men feel pain; I only uncover the pain that they have buried within themselves. Men are always treating themselves to pleasure; and it is the nature of pleasure when so indulged in to turn into pain" (*The Pitted Face* 56).

There is yet another issue that stands behind the Russian and Lebanese authors' inability to overcome their infantile sadistic desires, usually developing into the Oedipus complex, which prompts the child to want to destroy what he possesses and loves. In a relationship that is built on the principle of possession, the subject destroys its object and himself, as it is impossible to possess "something sacrosanct, radically individual, and belonging to no man, but the self-in-God" (Wasiolek 1986, 154). This is why the two heroes furiously stab their wives with daggers. Pozdnyshev's crime satisfies Tolstoy's desire for revenge against all the women who brought him up after his mother's early death, as well as against his mother herself for leaving him so early. And Naimy's hero kills his wife after feeling that his overexcited body failed to submit to his mind, so he was at the point of crossing the boundary that he had drawn himself.

Ironically, the authors proved unable to apply the universal love for everything that they both preached to their personal lives. For them, love turned out to be too abstract and barely applicable to their real-life situations. It became impossible for Naimy and Tolstoy to apply such a huge and faceless concept in practice in the course of ordinary carnal contact (Pomerants 2015), and that is why they never achieved harmony in their sexual relationships.

Tolstoy's novel drew Naimy's attention because he shared the Russian philosopher's confrontational philosophy about love, sexual relationships, and marriage, so the Lebanese author deliberately imitated it in his own work. The two writers suffered from similar psychosexual preoccupations, and that is why, of all Tolstoy's works, Naimy selected *KS* as a model in particular.

If the views of the Russian hermit fed and reinforced Naimy's philosophical and sexual squeamishness, Tolstoy's undisputed literary talent and style together with his imitation of certain hallmark features of Russian literature gave Naimy's ideas literary form. *The Pitted Face* is significant for its ethics, morals, and philosophy. Like Tolstoy's latter writings, which criticized the idea of art for art's sake, Naimy's novel cannot be judged on the basis of aesthetic and entertainment criteria.

Naimy could "underscore his own humanism and psychological depth by describing himself as [someone] who had been brought up on the fine art [of Russian literature]" (Litvin 2011, 106). He adopted the "dialect of the spirit" that characterized Tolstoy's work, and he made al-'Arqash go through the same spiritual and moral sufferings and crises that Tolstoy's heroes experience. Like the Russian author, he judges the conduct of al-'Arqash by his rigid moral precepts and worldview, which constitute "the pictorial criterion governing the presentation of his fiction" (Moser 1996, 297).

The Pitted Face is also characterized by "monumental historicism" (Lukov 2008), which is when the life of a single person becomes connected to international global developments. This fictional structure is illustrated throughout Russian literature. For example, Tolstoy's major works include descriptions of panoramic scenes and the destinies of individuals.

Naimy's novel has an incomplete composition that forces readers to guess what really happened and to predict how future events will transpire. *The Pitted Face* does not have a happy ending, which is more typical of Western fiction. The novel concludes with the author's thoughts after the story is over. This structure is also characteristic of Tolstoy and other Russian authors (Lukov 2008). Thus, *The Pitted Face* introduced elements of Russian literature into the modern Arabic literature tradition through its imitation of Tolstoy's work.

My research also makes a contribution to the topic of the Arab-Russian "cultural nexus and the continuing provocativeness of the literary works it has inspired" (Litvin 2011, 101), which has been a subject of increasing interest in recent times. The Cold War and the Soviet "Iron Curtain" divided the scholars who specialized in "The-Arabs-and-the-West binarism" (Litvin 2011, 105) into two groups with strictly different academic positions and with barely any cross-disciplinary investigations.[9] An examination of the contributions of both sides will prove to be extremely beneficial, and the need to pursue studies in this area has been voiced during several recent academic conferences and meetings.[10]

This article provides a contribution to the scholarship on the history and development of the modern Arabic literary tradition. One important part of this tradition is translation, whose role continues to be underestimated (Scoville 2015). By reading the two novels analyzed in this study from a comparative perspective, we are also following the modern movement to contextualize literature within different transnational and global movements.

Notes

1. The correct transliteration of Naimy's name is Mikha'īl Nu'ayma. But he spelled his name in English as Naimy (Naimy 1967, 68, ref. 1).

2. Mikha'il Naimy, *Sab'un: ḥikāyat 'umr* [Seventy: My life's story]. Hereafter, Sab.

3. Although Naseeb 'Areedah has imitated Russian poetry (1949).

4. Sofia Tolstaya exclaimed after reading her husband's diary: "There is quite an apparent thread that connects old Lëvochka's [Lev Tolstoy's] diaries with *The Kreuzer Sonata*!" (Shorè, cited in Voronina 2015, 27).

5. In Sab I, Naimy described with a lot of bitterness about cruel entertainment of boys, including himself, of his native village, who ruined birds' nests and killed and burned nestles. Tolstoy, in his works about vegetarianism, wrote about sufferings of killed animals at farms.

6. Even in classical antiquity, cuckolds were often considered to be physically or sexually impotent, or otherwise they would not have let their wives be unfaithful to them in the first place. Note, for example, the stock character of the *senex amans*, such as Januarie in Chaucer's *The Merchant's Tale*.

7. Our other literary archetype for this story is the narrative of how Joseph resisted Potiphar's wife in Genesis.

8. Again, the Old Testament provides a good story about this particular taboo: Genesis 31:35. Rachel is able to hide the stolen idols from her father, Laban, by sitting on the camel's saddle and claiming that she is having her period. It was taboo for any man to search where she was sitting.

9. The beginning of this separation could date to the postrevolutionary period, and not to the immediate postcolonial period, as Litvin (2011) claims.

10. Specifically, at the Boston University workshop on Arab-Russian ties, February 17–18, 2017, http://www.bu.edu/wll/news/bu-arab-russian-workshop/.

References

Beikham, Vandalen. 2016. *Ėntsiklopediia oruzhiia*. May 9. http://annales.info/evrope/behaym/behaym.htm.

Bilyk, I. E. 1984. "Tvorcheskiĭ metod Mikhaila Nuaime." PhD dissertation, Moscow State University.

Bloom, Harold. 1997. *The Anxiety of Influence: A Theory of Poetry*. Oxford: Oxford University Press.

———. 2011. *The Anatomy of Influence: Literature as a Way of Life*. New Haven, CT: Yale University Press.

Cruise, Edwina. 2002. "Women, Sexuality and the Family in Tolstoy." In *The Cambridge Companion to Tolstoy*, ed. Donna Tussing Orwin, 191–205. Cambridge: Cambridge University Press.

Dolinina, Anna. 2010. "Arabskiĭ Perevod Kreytserovoĭ Sonaty L. N. Tolstogo (Kair 1904)." *Arabeski : [izbrannye nauchnye stat'i]*. Sankt-Peterburg: Nestor-Istoriia: 290–96.

Ḥāfiẓ, Ṣabrī. 1997. *The Genesis of Arabic Narrative Discourse: A Study in the Sociology of Modern Arabic Literature*. London: Saqi Books.

Imangulieva, Aida Näsir qızı. 1975. *"Assotsiatsiia pera" i Mikhail Nuaime*. Moscow: Nauka.

———. 1986. "Russkaia literaturnaia i kriticheskaia mysl' i tvorchestvo Mikhaila Nuaime." *Shărg filologiĭasy măsălălări = Voprosy vostochnoi filologii.* Ed. Rustam M. Aliev. Baku: "Elm" năshriĭĭaty: 3–48.

———. 1991. *Korifei novoarabskoi literatury: K probleme vzaimosviazi literatur Vostoka i Zapada nachala XX veka.* Baku: Elm.

———. 2009. *Gibran, Rihani and Naimy: East–West Interactions in Early Twentieth-Century Arabic Literature.* Oxford: Inner Farne Press.

Litvin, Margaret. 2011. "Egypt's Uzbek Mirror: Muammad al-Mansi Qandil's Post-Soviet Islamic Humanism." *Journal of Arabic Literature* 42, no. 2–3: 101–19.

Lukov, Vladimir. 2008. "Osnovnye osobennosti russkoi literatury." *Filologiia* 5, http://www.zpu-journal.ru/e-zpu/2008/5/Lukov_russian_literature.

McLean, Hugh. 2008. *In Quest of Tolstoy.* Boston: Academic Studies Press.

Meyer, Priscilla. 2010. *How the Russians Read the French: Lermontov, Dostoevsky, Tolstoy.* Madison: University of Wisconsin Press.

Moser, Charles. 1996. *The Cambridge History of Russian Literature.* Cambridge: Cambridge University Press.

Naimy, Mikhail. 1952. *Memoirs of a Vagrant Soul* or *The Pitted Face.* New York: Philosophical Library.

———. 1979. *Sab'un: hikāyat 'umr* [Seventy: My life's story], 3 vols., in *Mikha'il Nu'aymah. Al-Majmū'ah Al-Kāmilah,* Vol. 1. Beirut: Dār Al-'Ilm lil-Malāyyin.

Naimy, Nadeem N. 1967. *Mikhail Naimy: An Introduction.* Publication of the Faculty of Arts and Sciences. Oriental Series 47. Beirut: American University of Beirut.

———. 1985. *The Lebanese Prophets of New York.* Beirut: American University of Beirut.

Nordau, Max. 1993. *Degeneration.* Lincoln: University of Nebraska Press.

Pomerants, Grigorii. *Vokrug rukopisi Stavrogina i "Kreitserovoi sonaty": Iz vstrech s Dostoevskim, chast' 1.* Accessed August 9, 2015. http://levi.ru/article.php?id_catalog=58&id_position=349.

Qubayn, Selim. 1904. *al-Wifāq wa al-Ṭalāq aw Lyahn Kritetsner. Ta'līf al-Faylasūf Leon Tolstoy.* Cairo: N.p.

Ramadan, Hadia Ihsan Hallak. 1993. "The Development of the Hero in Mikhail Naimy's Novels." MA thesis, American University in Cairo.

Rancour-Laferriere, Daniel. 1998. *Tolstoy on the Couch: Misogyny, Masochism and the Absent Mother.* London: Palgrave Macmillan.

Scoville, Spencer. 2015. "Reconsidering *Nahdawi* Translation: Bringing Pushkin to Palestine." *Translator* 21, no. 2: 223–26.

Tolstoy, Leo. *Izbrannye dnevniki, 1847–1894.* Accessed June 9, 2015, http://www.100bestbooks.ru/files/Tolstoy_Izbrannye_dnevniki.pdf.

———. 1928. *Tri dnia v derevne. Polnoe sobranie sochinenii,* vol. 28, 5–22. Moscow: Gos. izd-vo khudozh. lit-ry.

———. 1987. "Kreitserova Sonata." *Sobranie sochinenii v dvenadtcati tomakh.* Moscow: Pravda, vol. 11, 97–173.

———. 1982. "Posleslovie k Kreitserovoi Sonate." *Sobranie sochinenii v dvadtsati dvukh tomakh.* Moscow: Khudozhestvennaia literatura, vol. 12, 197–211.

Voronina, O. A. 2015. "'Kreitserova Sonata' L. N. Tolstogo kak vyrazhenie ego èticheskoi doktriny pola i zhenstvennosti." Accessed May 31. http://iph.ras.ru/uplfile/philec/kreizerova-sonata.pdf.

Wasiolek, Edward. 1986. "Why Does Anna Kill Herself?" In *Critical Essays on Tolstoy*, ed. Edward Wasiolek, 156–58. Boston: G. K. Hallpp.

The Role of Translation in Developing Arabic

■

Shehdeh Fareh, University of Sharjah, UAE

This study evaluates the impact of translation on Arabic. It also identifies the linguistic aspects that may be influenced by translation and determines whether these influences are signs of development or decay in the language. Specifically, the study aims at answering the following questions: (1) What is the role of translation in developing the Arabic language? (2) What aspects of language may change owing to the influence of translation? (3) How should the impact of translation on language be viewed? Is it development or decay? It was found that translation plays a positive effect in enriching Arabic, especially in the field of vocabulary. Finally, a number of recommendations are proposed.

Key words: Arabicization, borrowing, language contact, language change, language development, lexicography, morphological derivation, role of translation, translation

ملخص البحث

تهدف هذه الدراسة إلى توضيح أثر الترجمة على اللغة العربية وتحديد الجوانب اللغوية التي تتأثر سلباً أو ايجاباً بالترجمة من اللغة الإنجليزية إلى العربية. كما تسعى الدراسة إلى تقييم أثر الترجمة على اللغة العربية من حيث كونه تطوراً أو إفساداً للغة. وبالتحديد ستهدف الدراسة إلى الإجابة على الأسئلة الآتية: (1) ما دور الترجمة في تطور اللغة العربية، (2) ما الجوانب اللغوية التي قد تتأثر بالترجمة، (3) كيف ينبغي أن ننظر إلى أثر الترجمة على اللغة العربية؟ وأظهرت نتائج الدراسة أن الترجمة تلعب دوراً ايجابياً في إثراء العربية وبخاصة في مجال المفردات، وأخيراً قُدمت بعض التوصيات.

مقدمة

اللغة، في أبسط تعريف لها، وسيلة للتواصل بين البشر تتكون من نظام عام يتضمن مجموعة من الأنظمة الفرعية التي تحكمها قواعد النحو والصرف والصوت والدلالة. وهذه الظاهرة تتطور وتتغير بتطور حياة الناطقين بها. فهي تنمو وتزدهر بازدهار أهلها وتنحدر بانحدارهم ثقافياً وحضارياً وعلمياً وتكنولوجياً. ولذلك فاللغة مرآة تعكس واقع أهلها سلباً وإيجاباً وتتأثر بالظروف التي تستخدم فيها. فاللغة كما يصفها تمام حسان ظاهرة اجتماعية حية ووعاء للتجارب ودليل على النشاط الإنساني ومظهر السلوك اليومي الذي تقوم به الجماعة (2001:15). ويضيف حسان قائلاً: إن اللغة يجب أن تُدْرس وتُحلل وفقاً للمنهج الوصفي وليس التقريري وذلك عن طريق الملاحظة والوصف لما يقوله الناطقون بها ووضع القواعد له إذا ما أريد لهذه الدراسة أن تكون جدية ومنيعة. وفي ضوء هذه المنهجية الوصفية لا يجوز للباحث أن يكون متحيزاً في وصفه لآرائه الشخصية كأن يقول هذا يجوز وهذا لا يجوز (ص24) لأنه يصف ويحلل ما يلاحظه ويسمعه من اللغة المحكية حوله في فترة زمنية معينة. وهذا يعني أن اللغة تتغير من حين لآخر وفقاً للظروف التي يمر فيها أصحاب هذه اللغة ووفقاً لتفاعلهم الاجتماعي والاقتصادي والسياسي والثقافي والتكنولوجي مع الشعوب الأخرى الناطقة بلغات اخرى. وهناك عوامل كثيرة تؤدي إلى تطور اللغة سلباً أو إيجاباً سنوجزها فيما بعد.

أهداف الدراسة

تسعى هذه الدراسة إلى استقصاء دور الترجمة في تطوير اللغة العربية سواء أكان هذا التطور سلبياً أم إيجابياً. ولكي تحقق الدراسة هذا الهدف لا بد لها من التطرق باختصار إلى طبيعة اللغة من حيث التطور والجمود والتعرف على أسباب هذا التغير وتحديد الجوانب اللغوية التي يعتريها التغير عبر الزمن. وتركز الدراسة على دور الترجمة في تطور اللغة العربية ونموها في جوانب متعددة، ثم تخلص في النهاية إلى تقييم آثار الترجمة على اللغة العربية سلبية كانت أم إيجابية. وبالتحديد، تحاول هذه الدراسة تقديم إجابات للأسئلة الآتية:

1. ما دور الترجمة في تطوير اللغة العربية؟
2. ما هي الجوانب اللغوية التي يمكن أن يعتريها التغير بسبب الترجمة؟
3. هل التغير اللغوي تحسين ينبغي تشجيعه أم تدمير لا بد من محاربته واعتراض سبيله؟

أهمية الدراسة

تعزى أهمية هذه الدراسة إلى الأمور الآتية:

1. إن تحديد دور الترجمة من اللغات الأخرى، وبخاصة اللغة الإنجليزية، إلى اللغة العربية يكشف حقيقة هذه اللغة المتطورة المتغيرة القادرة على استيعاب روح العصر والتعبير عن اختراعاته وابتكاراته دون أن تظل جامدة وقاصرة عن التعبير عما يستجد من عبارات ومصطلحات علمية وسياسية واقتصادية وتكنولوجية .وشأنها في ذلك شأن سائر اللغات الحية.
2. تُبْرز هذه الدراسة الطاقات والقدرات الكامنة في اللغة العربية التي لم يحاول بعض الباحثين تطويرها بل تركوها مهملة دون استغلال سواء أكان ذلك عن قصد أو غير قصد حتى أصبح بعضهم يعُدّ هذه اللغة غير قادرة على تلبية حاجاتهم كوسيلة للتعبير عن مستجدات العصر ومبتكراته .كما اعتقد بعض هؤلاء الباحثين أن اللغة العربية قاصرة بطبيعتها وبنيتها ولا ترقى لمستوى اللغات الأخرى من حيث مرونتها وقدرتها على مواكبة المتطلبات الحضارية المعاصرة.
3. إن التركيز على دور الترجمة في تطوير اللغة العربية يبرز قدرة هذه اللغة على التطور المستمر والتفاعل الدائم مع شعوب العالم ومنتجاتهم الحضارية .ولذلك فإن التركيز على تفاعل اللغة العربية مع غيرها من اللغات والحضارات يدفع عنها تهمة العجز والقصور .وقد يعزى اتهام العربية بالقصور إلى عدة أسباب منها:

أ.عدم معرفة القائلين بهذا الاتهام بطبيعة اللغة العربية وقدرتها على الاشتقاق والصوغ ومرونتها في استيعاب مستجدات العصر العلمية والتكنولوجية.

ب. افتتان بعض الباحثين بالحضارة الغربية وبما هو جديد، أو بسبب توجهاتهم الفكرية والأيديولوجية.

ت .تجاهل بعض الباحثين حقيقة كون القصور والعجز في أي لغة لا يعزى إلى طبيعة اللغة نفسها، بل لأهلها والناطقين بها وما يمرون به من ظروف اقتصادية وسياسية وتكنولوجية تنعكس سلباً على لغتهم .وفي الواقع فإن كل لغة قادرة على الإيفاء بحاجات أهلها التواصلية والتعبيرية ما دام أهل اللغة حريصين على التطور والتفاعل مع اللغات والحضارات الأخرى .فكلما نشط أهل لغة وزودوها بمفردات جديدة عن طريق الاختراعات والابتكارات العلمية والترجمة والتعريب زادت تلك اللغة ثراءً وازدهاراً ونفت عن نفسها سمة العجز والقصور .ويصدق ذلك على اللغة العربية وأهلها في العصر الأموي والعباسي حيث اتسعت رقعة الدولة الإسلامية واختلط العرب بشعوب أخرى واطلعوا على علومهم وترجموا العديد من الكتب في مجالات الطب والعلوم المختلفة، مما أدى إلى تطور علم الطب لديهم بعد أن كان يعتمد على الطب النبوي وعلى الأعشاب والنباتات الطبية، فتطورت ممارسة الطب عند العرب وأضافوا لما كان لديهم من معرفة رصينة عن طريق ترجمة كتب الطب من اللغات اليونانية والهندية والسريانية.

4. إن إبراز دور الترجمة يذكرنا بدورها في تطوير البحث العلمي في مجالات العلوم المختلفة وبخاصة في عصرنا الحاضر الذي يعاني فيه العالم العربي والإسلامي من تأخر علمي وتكنولوجي مقارنة بالدول الغربية التي تشهد سباقاً محموماً في البحث العلمي والتقدم التكنولوجي في ميادين الحياة المختلفة .وفي مثل هذه الظروف تؤدي الترجمة دوراً مهماً في نقل أنواع مختلفة من العلوم والتقنيات إلى اللغة العربية.
5. ولعل الترجمة من أهم وسائل معرفة الآخرين للتفاعل الثقافي والحضاري معهم، الأمر الذي يؤدي إلى الارتقاء بالذات وتطويرها واتضاح الفكر وتشعيب العلوم وتطورها .ولذلك فالترجمة هي الأساس في عملية التواصل والتجسير المعرفي والثقافي والعلمي والحضاري بين الأمم.
6. أدت الترجمة أيضاً رسالة إيجابية في تنقية أسلوب الكتابة العربية من التكلف والتنميق والتركيز على المبنى على حساب المعنى في عصور الضعف والانحطاط .وقد تحقق ذلك بفضل الترجمات

من اللغات الأخرى إلى اللغة العربية التي حرص مترجموها على نقل المعنى والرسالة اللغوية بشكل مفيد دون الاهتمام بالشكل أو المبنى اللغوي فقط.

7. تتميز المعرفة الإنسانية بالتراكمية وتعمل الترجمة على نقل التراث العلمي والإبداع الفكري من أمة إلى أخرى .وقد أدركت دول العالم المعاصرة أهمية الترجمة في تطوير لغاتها وحضارتها فأولت هذه العملية أهمية كبيرة ونشطت في مجال ترجمة العلوم بمختلف أنواعها.

وخلاصة القول إن الترجمة مفتاح للاطلاع على ثقافات الأمم الأخرى وحضاراتها والإفادة من إبداعاتها وإنتاجها الفكري وبخاصة في هذا العصر الذي لم تعد فيه المعرفة حكراً على أحد، ولا يتطلب الحصول عليها عناء كبيراً. إن التغيرات التي تحدثها الترجمة في اللغات المستهدفة لا ينكرها أحد. ولا بد لنا في هذا المقام أن نستعرض بإيجاز أسباب التغير اللغوي لنركز على دور الترجمة على وجه الخصوص بصفتها عاملاً فاعلاً في التطور اللغوي.

أسباب التغير اللغوي

تتعرض اللغة إلى التغير والتطور باستمرار ولكن هذا التغير يكون بطيئاً لا نكاد نشعر به. واللغة العربية خضعت للتغير والتطور شأنها في ذلك شأن جميع لغات العالم. فقد مرت اللغة العربية في مراحل متعددة من التطور. فالعربية المعاصرة تختلف عن لغة الشعر الجاهلي، وتختلف عن لغة القرآن والحديث، فهي لغة تشترك مع لغة الشعر الجاهلي ولغة القرآن والحديث في جوانب كثيرة وتختلف عنهما في جوانب أخرى كما يقول تمام حسان (2001:182).

ويعزى هذا التغير إلى أسباب كثيرة أهمها ما ذكره أرلوتو(Arlotto 1972:149–84) وباينون(Bynon 1983:123–67) وهدسون (Hudson 2000:398–95) حيث تحدث هؤلاء اللغويون عن أسباب التغير في النظام الصوتي والصرفي والنحوي والدلالي للغة الإنجليزية. ومعظم الأسباب التي ذكروها تنطبق على اللغات الأخرى. ومن أهم هذه الأسباب ما يأتي:

1. الرغبة في التجديد والتعبير عن معنى جديد حيث إن ظاهرة انفتاح اللغة ومرونتها تسمح للناطقين بها باختراع كلمات جديدة للتعبير عن أشياء أو ابتكارات أو أفكار جديدة في مجالات التكنولوجيا والطب والأعمال والاقتصاد
2. إخضاع الصيغ غير القياسية إلى القياس
3. هجر بعض المعاني وعدم استعمال مفرداتها
4. التّماس الذي يحدث بين اللغات عندما يجد الناطقون بلغات مختلفة أنفسهم مضطرين للتواصل معاً مما يؤدي إلى كثير من الاقتراض بين اللغات. فعلى سبيل المثال، فإن ما يقرب من 60%من مفردات اللغة الإنجليزية تعود إلى أصول لاتينية وفرنسية ويونانية وإسبانية (Hudson 2000:392–95)
5. الترجمة والتعريب :تعد الترجمة من أكبر عوامل التغيير في اللغات وبخاصة فيما يتعلق بالمفردات .فقد أدخلت الترجمة إلى العربية مئات الكلمات الجديدة التي لم تكن موجودة أصلاً فيها في مجالات عديدة كالطب والفلسفة والاقتصاد والسياسة والإعلام، كما سنوضح فيما يأتي:

دور الترجمة في تطوير اللغة العربية

لقد كان للترجمة تأثيرات متنوعة على جوانب مختلفة من اللغة العربية. وكان أبرز تأثير للترجمة في المفردات سواء أكان ذلك عن طريق الترجمة أو التعريب أو الاشتقاق. كما أثرت الترجمة أيضاً على النظام الصرفي والنحوي والدلالي والأسلوبي. وسنوضح تأثير الترجمة على كل جانب من هذه الجوانب بإيجاز وعدد محدود من الأمثلة. وسنبيِّن ما إذا كان هذا التأثير سلبياً أو إيجابياً. ويتضح تأثير الترجمة على اللغة العربية في الجوانب السبعة الآتية:

1. التعريب

لقد دخلت إلى العربية مفردات أجنبية كثيرة بعد أن خضعت لعملية تطبيع من حيث إخضاعها لقواعد النظام الصوتي والصرفي، فغدت هذه المفردات كأنها من أصل عربي لا يكاد كثير من الناس يقبل التشكيك في عروبتها. ومن هذه المفردات: أكاديمية، بوليسية، استوديو، كوافير، فيلم، بنك، ديموقراطية، بيروقراطية، تكنولوجيا، كمبيوتر، تلفزيون، راديو، الإثنية، الجندرية، اللوجستية، رالي، أولمبياد، فلسفة، هرطقة، كنفيدرالية، أجندة، مونديال، سيناريو، استراتيجية، ديناميكي، دراما، إنفلونزا، بانوراما، معكرونة، بنطلون، باروكة، إنترنت، إيميل، تليفون، تلغراف، سوسيولوجي، سيكولوجية، دكتاتورية، الإمبريالية، أنثروبولوجيا، السيميائية، مغناطيس، إلكترون، إلكترونيات، تلسكوب، موديل، هيدروكربونات، أتمتة، مكننة، لا انطباقية، إيكولوجيا، بيولوجيا، جينوم، جين، بروتوكل، كاريزما، لا أدرية، برجوازية، برلمان، كاثوليكية، كليشيه، كوميديا، فاشي، فانتازيا، سينما، أيقونة، مايكروويف، أدرينالين، الغوريتم، ليبرالية، ميتافيزيقا، بوليمرات، بلاستيك، سليلوز، أنزيم، ميكروسكوب، الكترومغناطيسي، زيجوت، جالون ،الصواريخ البالستية، رادار، وغيرها كثير.

ومما لا شك فيه أن هذه المفردات ومثيلاتها الكثيرة أثْرت المعجم العربي وأضافت إليه ما لم يكن فيه وأصبحت دارجة مستساغة ومقبولة للذوق اللغوي العام، وبذلك كان تأثيرها إيجابياً على المخزون اللغوي العربي. ويعزى سبب اقتراض هذه المفردات إلى أسباب متعددة أهمها حاجة اللغة العربية لمثل هذه المفردات لسد ثغرات معجمية. فقد وجدت هذه المفردات في لغاتها الأصلية لتصف أشياء وابتكارات وأفكاراً وعلوماً وتقنيات وظواهر لم تكن في معظمها موجودة في الثقافة العربية، ولهذا تم اقتراضها وتعريبها. كما أن التبادل الثقافي والتفاعل بين العرب وغيرهم من الأمم من خلال التجارة والمجاورة والتعايش المشترك بين الشعوب التي تتضمن إثنيات متنوعة أدّى إلى اقتراض مثل هذه المفردات للتعبير عن معان غير موجودة أصلاً في العربية. ولا يقتصر هذا الجانب على تأثر اللغة العربية بغيرها فحسب بل يشمل أيضاً تأثير هذه اللغة على اللغات الأخرى. وإذا نظرنا إلى ما حدث لهذه المفردات عندما نقلت إلى العربية لوجدنا أنها خضعت لعملية تطبيع وإخضاع وتغيير لتنسجم مع قوانين النظام الصوتي والنظام الصرفي وقواعد الاشتقاق في اللغة العربية حيثما تطلب الأمر ذلك. فمثلاً تحول الصوت الذي يمثله الحرف /p/في اللغة الإنجليزية إلى أقرب نظير له وهو صوت حرف /ب/في العربية، كما في كلمة بوليس "police" وكمبيوتر "computer" وأنثروبولوجيا "anthropology". وهناك استراتيجية ثانية أبقت على لفظ بعض المفردات كما هو تقريباً في الحالات التي لا يتعارض فيها نطق تلك الكلمات الأجنبية مع النظام الصوتي العربي كما في الكلمات فيلم "film" ودراما "drama" وجين"gene" ومن هذه الكلمات ما صيغ على وزن من الأوزان القياسية العربية المعروفة وهو وزن 'فعللة' كما في المفردات أتمتة ومكننة.

وأما الألفاظ الأجنبية التي تنتهي بلاحقة تفيد معنى الاسم (اسم علم أو ظاهرة) مثل "-logy" و "-ship" و "-ism" كما في "anthropology" و "dictatorship" و "imperialism" فقد خضعت أولاً

لتطبيع صوتي باستبدال الأصوات غير الموجودة في العربية بأقرب نظيراتها في العربية ثم أضيف لها لاحقة مثل التاء المربوطة كما في ديمقراطية ودكتاتورية أو الألف الممدودة كما في أنثروبولوجيا وبيولوجيا وتكنولوجيا. ولسنا في هذا المجال بصدد التفصيل في العمليات الفونولوجية التي تخضع لها المفردات الأجنبية المعربة أو المقترضة.

وذكرت الباحثة زينب إبراهيم (2006) في استعراضها لموضوع الاقتراض في اللغة العربية من اللغات الأخرى وبخاصة في اللغة المكتوبة أسباب الاقتراض ومجالاته. وقالت إن اللغة تضطر لاقتراض مفردات من لغة أخرى عندما يحدث احتكاك ثقافي بين الناطقين بلغات مختلفة، لعدم احتوائها على المفردات المُقترَضة التي تملأ فراغاً في اللغة المستقبِلة أو لأن المفردات الجديدة ترتبط بسمعة عالية أو لأنها تسميات لمخترعات وتقنيات أجنبية. وقد تضمنت ميادين الاقتراض الاعلانات التجارية والفنون والألعاب الرياضية والموضات وبعض الجوانب الزراعية والصناعية والتقنية والشؤون الداخلية للبلاد. وأوردت الباحثة أمثلة كثيرة للمفردات التي دخلت إلى اللغة العربية في الصحف المصرية وبخاصة صحيفة الأهرام، ومن هذه المفردات: تليفون، بيجاما، سوبرلوكس، أسانسيرات، موبيليات، ديكورات، موكيت، سيراميك، صالونات، شاليه، كاسيت، موتور، راديو، بطارية، بنطلون، جينز، فيلم، فيديو، بلاستيك، أوكازيون، بيتزا، دبلوم، بنك، كافتيريا، أوبرا، تنس، فستان، إسمنت، ميكروفون وإنترنت.

2. اشتقاق الأفعال من الأسماء المعرَّبة

لم يقتصر تأثير الترجمة على إضافة مفردات فحسب، بل أثرت على عملية الاشتقاق أيضاً. فقد خضع الكثير من المفردات المعربة لقوانين اشتقاق الأفعال من الأسماء قياساً على بعض الأوزان العربية. يقول عصفور: "اشتقاق الأفعال ممكن من الأسماء الأجنبية إذا كان الفعل الناتج رباعياً وغير ممكن في الحالات الأخرى" (2007: 199)، كما حدث في الأفعال "تلفن" و"تلفز" و"أكسد" و "هدرج" و "أدلج" (من "أيديولوجيا" "وهرطق" وكربن وسمر (ينوم مغناطيسياً) وغيرها.

ومن قبيل الاشتقاق ما حدث في الكلمات الأجنبية التي تتكون من سابقة/لاصقة متصلة بجذر. وقد تكون الكلمة الناتجة مقبولة أو غير مقبولة في بعض الحالات. ومن اللواصق التي دخلت إلى العربية وأصبحت مقبولة اللاصقة "لا" كما في: اللانهائي واللاأخلاقي واللاأدرية واللافلزية واللامنهجية واللاصفية ولا إرادي واللاديني واللاوعي واللاإنسانية واللامساوة واللاسامية واللاتوافق واللاحكم واللادستورية. وكذلك السابقة "ما" كما يقول عصفور (2007: 199) في المفردات: الماورائية والماتريدية. ويعزو عصفور سبب قبول هاتين السابقتين "إلى وجود معنى لهما في حالتي الاتصال والانفصال على السواء" (2007: 199).

ويبدو أن القائمين على إعداد المعاجم لم يوفقوا في ترجمة العديد من السوابق ولذلك لم تغادر تلك الكلمات مواقعها في المعاجم كما ورد في قاموس المورد في ترجمة السابقة "-inter" إلى "بيـ-" في العربية مثل بيسني "interdental" وبيدائري "interdepartmental" وبيثقافي "intercultural" وبيقاري -inter" "continental، ولكن قاموس أطلس الموسوعي لم يعتمد ترجمة هذه السابقة بهذا الشكل، بل استخدم الكلمة العربية المستقلة "بين" للتعبير عن السابقة الإنجليزية "-inter" كما في المفردات: بين سني و بين قاري وبين الأقسام بدلاً من "بيدائري" في قاموس المورد.

ومن السوابق التي لم تلق ترجمتها أذنا صاغية ولم يقبلها الذوق اللغوي ما ورد في قاموس المورد في ترجمة السابقة "—post"، كما ترجمت في الكلمات: بعديْحربي "postwar" و بعديولادتي -postna" "tal، وبعديجراحي "postoperative" وبعديوليمي "postprandial" وبعديزواجي "postnuptial" وبعديعلّي "postvocalic"، وبعديدكتوراتي "postdoctoral". ولم يتبنَّ قاموس أطلس ترجمة هذه السابقة كما وردت في المورد، بل ترجمها إلى الكلمة العربية "بعد" أو "خلف": حادث بعد الحرب وبعد الولادة وبعد الجراحة ولاحق لوجبة وواقع بعد الزواج، وهكذا.

ولعل السبب الذي حفز البعلبكي لتكوين كلمات كالمذكورة أعلاه هو الرغبة في ترجمة كلمة بكلمة مما أدى إلى إنتاج تلك الكلمات التي يصعب نطقها أحياناً ناهيك عن سهولة استخدامها ومدى شيوعها. والسؤال الذي يُطرح هنا: ما العيب أو الخطأ في ترجمة كلمة أجنبية بأكثر من كلمة واحدة في اللغة العربية؟ فالتكافؤ التام بين اللغات يكاد يكون مستحيلاً وبخاصة في مجال المفردات التي يكون لبعضها خصوصية ثقافية وليس لها مكافئ من كلمة واحدة في اللغة الأخرى.

ومن السوابق الأخرى التي ترجمت بشكل لا يروق للذوق العربي ما أورده البعلبكي (2007) في قاموس المورد من ترجمة للسابقة "-under" كما في الكلمات تحذراعي "underarm" وتحأرضي "underground" وتحبحري "undersea" وتحمائي "underwater". ولكن قاموس المورد لا يطبق قاعدة إلصاق السابقة بالجذر على جميع المفردات المشابهة. فمثلاً يترجم المورد كلمات "postmeridian"بـ "بعد الظهر" و كلمة "postmortem" بـ "بعد الموت" و "postclassical" بـ "بعد عصر كلاسيكي".

ولا شك أن هذه العملية خطوة جريئة في مجال نحت كلمات جديدة للتعبير عن معاني كلمات أجنبية تتكون من لاصقة واحدة أو أكثر بالإضافة إلى جذر الكلمة. هناك أمران يحددان مدى قبول مثل هذه المفردات أو رفضها، وبشكل أدق مدى شيوعها أو بقائها رهينة المعجم وهما:

(1) مدى انسجام الكلمة الجديدة مع الصيغ أو الأوزان العربية المألوفة .فكلما اتفقت الكلمة مع هذه الأوزان زاد شيوعها واستخدامها، وإلا تظل الكلمة حبيسة ونادرة الاستخدام.

(2) سهولة قراءتها ونطقها :لاحظنا أن المرء يتوقف لحظات قبل أن يستطيع نطق بعض المفردات التي أوردها المورد .كما يحتاج القارئ إلى فترة طويلة نوعاً ما إلى معالجة هذه المفردات ذهنياً لكي يتمثل معانيها ويستوعبها مثل :بعديولادي و بعديعلي وبعديحربي وبعديدكتوراتي وغيرها.

3. الترجمة المباشرة "Calquing"

تُعرَّف الترجمة المباشرة بأنها ترجمة الكلمة أو العبارة الأجنبية ترجمة مباشرة لكل مورفيم فيها إلى ما يقابله مباشرة في لغة أخرى، وبذلك فإن الترجمة تعكس معنى العبارة الأجنبية تماماً. وبمعنى آخر فالترجمة المباشرة تعني ترجمة الكلمة بكلمة أخرى أو عبارة بالعبارة التي تقابلها في اللغة الهدف مثل ناطحة سحاب "skyscraper" وشهر العسل "honeymoon" وغسل الدماغ "brainwash" والحرب الباردة "cold war" والحرب الخاطفة "lightning war" وغيرها. فإذا نظرنا إلى هذه العبارات العربية نجد أنها لم تكن معروفة في اللغة العربية ولكنها دخلت إليها عن طريق الترجمة المباشرة لمكونات العبارة الأجنبية. وبلا شك فقد عملت الترجمة المباشرة على إثراء المعجم العربي بمئات المفردات والعبارات التي لا يكاد المرء يصدق أنها دخيلة ومن أصل غير عربي.

يذكر علي (2005) في مقالة له باللغة الإنجليزية بعنوان: "الترجمة المباشرة: وسيلة لإثراء اللغة" إنه يمكن اعتبار الترجمة المباشرة نوعاً من الاقتراض بين اللغات حيث تكيف اللغة المقترضة نفسها لتستوعب كلمة أو عبارة جديدة بإيجاد مفردات مكافئة لعناصر العبارة الأجنبية. ويضيف علي قائلاً: "إن هذا النوع من الاقتراض يملأ فراغاً في اللغة المقترِضة عندما لا تحتوي هذه اللغة مفردة أو عبارة للتعبير عن مفهوم جديد" (2005: 116). وتزداد هذه العملية بازدياد التفاعل الثقافي بين الشعوب. ويميز علي (2005) بين سبعة أنواع من الترجمة المباشرة المستخدمة في اللغة العربية لنقل مفاهيم جديدة من اللغات الأخرى وبخاصة من اللغة الإنجليزية. وسنوضح هذه الاستراتيجيات السبع باختصار فيما يأتي:

أ. الترجمة المباشرة كلمة كلمة: تتضح هذه الإستراتيجية في الأمثلة الآتية:

1. غسل/تبييض الأموال "money laundering"
2. غسل الدماغ "brainwash"

3. انفجار سكاني "population explosion"
4. يلقي الضوء على "shed light on"
5. وصلت إلى طريق مسدود "reached an impasse"

نلاحظ أن هذه الترجمات ترجمة مباشرة، كلمة كلمة للعبارات التي تقابلها في اللغة الإنجليزية، ولكن هذه الترجمة قد تكون جزئية أحياناً كما في النوع الثاني.

ب. الترجمة الجزئية: يحدث في هذه الاستراتيجية تعديل طفيف على بعض أجزاء العبارة الأجنبية لغرض معين كما في العبارة "ناطحة سحاب" "skyscraper" في الإنجليزية. فبدلاً من ترجمة "sky" بكلمة "السماء" استخدمت كلمة "السحاب" لأسباب دينية تتعلق بمعنى كلمة السماء في العربية. والعبارة "استقبال/ترحيب حار" "warm reception/welcome" تقدم مثالاً آخر استخدمت فيه كلمة "حار" "hot" بدلاً من دافئ "warm" لتنسجم مع الميل للمبالغة في الترحيب في الثقافة العربية.

ت. التغير الدلالي في معنى المفردة أو العبارة "semantic shift" : تتضمن هذه الاستراتيجية إضافة جانب من جوانب معنى العبارة الأجنبية إلى الكلمة العربية التي لم يكن ذلك الجانب جزءاً من معناها كما في الأمثلة الآتية:

1. قطار "train" أصلها "caravan"
2. تصفية "Liquidation" ولكن "تصفية" تعني أصلاً "purification, filtration"

ويمكن اعتبار هذا النوع من الترجمة اتساعا في مدلولات المفردة العربية.

ث. نحت كلمات جديدة للتعبير عن مفهوم أجنبي: فعلى سبيل المثال، ترجمت كلمة "homo- sexuals" بكلمة "المثليون" التي عبرت عن معنى السابقة الإنكليزية "-homo" التي تعنى "مثل" ثم صيغت منها كلمة "مثليون". ومن الأمثلة الأخرى فضائيات "space channels" وحاسوب بدلاً من "computer" ومرمدة "ashtray".

ج. العبارات المركبة: وهي ترجمة حرفية كلمة كلمة للعبارات الإنكليزية كما يظهر في الأمثلة الآتية:

أجسام مضادة "antibodies"
حارس المرمى "goalkeeper"
وزن الذبابة "flyweight"
الأغلبية الساحقة "overwhelming majority"
الأشغال الشاقة "hard labor"
أسلحة الدمار الشامل "mass destruction weapons"
السبورة الذكية "smart board"
كأس العالم "World Cup"
القرص المدمج "compact disc"

ح. العبارات الهجينة "Hybrid Calques": قد يحدث أحياناً أن تتضمن العبارة العربية كلمة من أصل عربي مكافئة لإحدى كلمات العبارة الأجنبية بحيث تبقى الكلمة الأخرى باللغة الأجنبية بعد تعريبها كما في الأمثلة الآتية:

مقياس ريختر "Richter scale"
مقهى الإنترنت "internet café"
الحصانة الدبلوماسية "diplomatic immunity"
مقابلة تلفزيونية "television interview"

خ. المختصرات: وهي كلمات تتكون من الحروف الأولى لكلمتين أو أكثر كما في الأمثلة الآتية:
الناتو: منظمة حلف شمال الأطلسي "NATO: North Atlantic Treaty Organization"
الرادار: "RADAR: Radio Detection and Ranging"

إن هذه الأنواع المختلفة من الترجمة تشير بوضوح إلى الدور الذي تلعبه الترجمة في إثراء اللغة المستقبِلة و بخاصة في مجال المفردات و المصطلحات. ويمكننا القول إن عملية الترجمة المباشرة كلمة كلمة "Calqu-ing" بجميع انواعها المذكورة آنفاً أصبحت شائعة الاستعمال في اللغة العربية المعاصرة وبدأت تحل محل الاقتراض اللغوي أو التعريب تدريجياً. فهي استراتيجية تثري المخزون اللغوي العربي بطريقة تنسجم والأنظمة الصرفية والاشتقاقية والصوتية للغة العربية. وهذا ما يجعل هذه الإضافات مألوفة للقارئ العربي إلى الحد الذي لا يدفعنا للتفكير في أنها مترجمة من اللغة الانجليزية وبشكل لا تثير معه ريبة القارئ العربي ولا تجذب الانتباه إلى أنها ترجمات من اللغة الإنجليزية. و لذلك ينبغي أن نشجع هذا التوجه كوسيلة لإثراء المفردات والمصطلحات العربية ودليل على مرونة اللغة العربية في تفاعلها مع اللغات الأخرى.

4. أثر الترجمة الإعلامية على اللغة العربية

تعد وسائل الإعلام المختلفة من أهم العوامل التي تسهم في تشكيل الثقافة في المجتمع. ولكن أثرها لا يقتصر على الثقافة فحسب بل يتعداه إلى التأثير على اللغة نفسها. ومن وظائف الإعلام والصحافة ما يسمى بالوظيفة اللغوية التي تعمل فيها وسائل الإعلام على تطوير اللغة وتحديثها وإثرائها بالمفردات والعبارات الجديدة إما بنشرها وترسيخها أو "بإقصائها وإخفائها وإيجاد بدائل لها" كما يقول الجبر (661 :2009). ولوسائل الإعلام قدرة هائلة على صياغة مفردات جديدة عن طريق التعريب والترجمة ومن ثم نشرها وترسيخها بين الناس. وما يعزز ذلك كثرة وسائل الإعلام وسهولة انتشارها بين الناس. ويمكن تلخيص أثر الترجمة الإعلامية على اللغة العربية في ثلاثة مجالات: الكتابة الإعلامية، وتعريب المصطلحات، ونحت المفردات والمختصرات.

أ. الكتابة الإعلامية:

أثرت الترجمة على طريقة صياغة الجمل وبخاصة عناوين الصحف، فأصبحت عناوين الصحف وعناوين الأخبار تبدأ بالاسم بدلاً من الفعل كما هو الحال في النمط الشائع في الجمل العربية. كما أن صياغة هذه العناوين تكون بطريقة جذابة ولافتة كما هو الحال في عناوين الصحف الإنجليزية. وعلاوة على ذلك نلاحظ أن بنية القصة الإخبارية تأثرت بأسلوب كتابة الخبر في اللغة الإنجليزية. يبدأ الخبر بجملة قصيرة موجزة تلخص الحدث أو القصة ثم يتبعها تفاصيل الخبر على غرار القصة الإخبارية في الصحف الإنجليزية. ويعود ذلك إلى أن الفقرة الإنجليزية تتكون من جملة موجزة تلخص موضوع الفقرة ثم يليها عدد من الجمل التي تفصّل موضوع ما ذكر بإيجاز في العنوان. ولعل ذلك يعزى إلى تأثير الترجمة من اللغة الإنجليزية إلى العربية. ونحن نجد، إذا ما تصفحنا جريدة عربية، جزءاً كبيراً منها مترجماً. ولم يعرف العرب الكتابة الصحفية إلا في فترة متأخرة بعدما كانت الصحف الأجنبية قد قطعت شوطاً طويلاً في هذا المضمار. والأمثلة الآتية توضح هذا التأثير:

"زلزال إيران يهز المنطقة ولا خسائر في الإمارات، الإمارات تدين انفجارات بوسطن، المجلس الاستشاري يناقش غداً سياسة القيادة العامة. . . .، تثمين ليبي لدعم الإمارات، بحث علاقات التعاون مع اليابان، بيونغ يانغ تهدد سيؤول مجدداً، الصين تؤكد أولوية الدفاع عن سيادتها".

(جريدةالخليج 2013/4/17 العدد 12386)

ب. تعريب المصطلحات:

كما أن الترجمة الإعلامية أدخلت كلمات كثيرة إلى اللغة العربية في المجال الإعلامي عن طريق تعريب بعض المصطلحات والعبارات وتطبيعها وفقاً لنظام الأصوات العربية. ويظهر هذا الأثر واضحاً في العديد من العبارات المستخدمة في الصحف ووسائل الإعلام الأخرى مثل الإثنية والجندرية واللوجستية والسياسة الناعمة والعولمة والبلقنة والسعودة، والبريسترويكا والتجسير وحرب الاستنزاف والبرمجة والدبلجة والمأسسة والعولمة والاستنساخ وغسيل الأموال والتطبيع والعسكرة والأنسنة والمؤللة (المساكن المؤللة: مساكن صُمِّمت على شكل الآلات التي نستخدمها) والدوريات المؤللة (دوريات تدعمها آليات عسكرية)، والأرشيف (مكان حفظ الوثائق)، وتسونامي وإسلام فوبيا، وسوق الأوراق المالية وسياسة القطب الواحد والضربات الاستباقية وغيرها. وما إن تظهر بعض هذه العبارات في الصحف وتتداول بين الناس وفي وسائل الإعلام المرئي حتى تشق طريقها في الاستخدام اللغوي وتصبح جزءاً لا يتجزأ من اللغة العربية، ولذلك فإن التعريب مصدر أساسي لإثراء اللغة بمفردات ومصطلحات جديدة في ميادين متنوعة.

وفي معرض الحديث عن إدخال عبارات مفردات جديدة إلى اللغة العربية من خلال الترجمة من اللغات الأجنبية إلى العربية، ذكر رمضان المغراب (2011) أن التعريب من أهم الأساليب التي أسهمت في تحديث اللغة العربية في مجال المفردات حيث يُعرِّف المغراب عملية التعريب بأنها "عملية ترجمة المفردات او العبارات الأجنبية باستخدام الحروف العربية" (2011: 496) كما حدث في نقل كلمة "philosophy" إلى "فلسفة" وكلمة "drachma" إلى "درهم" و "asphalt" إلى "إسفلت". ويضيف المغراب أن التعريب يحقق الأهداف الآتية: (1) الحفاظ على بقاء اللغة العربية وتطور مفرداتها، (2) إيجاد مفردات عربية ثابتة للمفردات العلمية والتقنية الأجنبية، (3) إحياء التراث الثقافي العربي الإسلامي. ويؤكد المغراب على أهمية التعريب بقوله إنه "وسيلة لإثراء اللغة العربية ومن خلاله تستعيد اللغة العربية دورها الريادي في عالمنا المعاصر" (2011: 496).

ومن الجدير بالذكر هنا أن المفردات المعرَّبة قد تخضع لبعض التغييرات الصوتية والكتابية لتتلاءم مع الأنظمة الصوتية والصرفية والكتابية للغة العربية كما يلاحظ في تعريب كلمة "oxidize" إلى "يؤكسد" التي اشتقت منها كلمات "أكسدة ومؤكسِد ومؤكسَد".

وخلص المغراب إلى القول إن التعريب أكثر فاعلية من الاشتقاق في إضافة مفردات جديدة إلى اللغة العربية.

ت. نحت المفردات والمختصرات:

ليست ظاهرة النحت جديدة أو دخيلة على اللغة العربية. فقد كانت معروفة عند القدامى، ولو بشكل محدود. وتعني هذه الكلمة القطع والنشر والاختزال والتنقيص كما ورد في المعاجم العربية مثل لسان العرب وتاج العروس. ويعني النحت بالمعنى الاصطلاحي، تكوين كلمة جديدة من حروف كلمتين أو كلمات متتالية كما في:

"حيعل" فعل اشتق من كلمتي "حيَّ" و "على"،

بسمل: اشتق من "بسم الله الرحمن الرحيم"،

حمدل: اشتق من الحمد لله،

عبشميّ: نسبة إلى عبد شمس،

وغيرها من المنحوتات. ومع ازدياد استعمال اللغة العربية في تدريس العلوم المعاصرة ازدادت الحاجة إلى المصطلحات والمختصرات المستعملة في هذه العلوم. ومن أهم الدوافع للنحت التوجه العام نحو الاختزال والاختصار والاقتصاد اللغوي في ميادين الحياة المختلفة. وهذا ما دفع ساطع الحصري في مقالة بعنوان "النحت" للقول: "لا يمكن نشر العلم بالتراكيب المطولة، فإذا لم نقبل النحت، سنضطر إلى استعمال الاصطلاحات الإفرنجية نفسها ولا حاجة لإثبات أن اتساق اللغة في هذه الحالة يصبح أشد تعرضاً للخطر" (95 :1985). وقد شجع الحصري على استخدام النحت واستعمله في كتاباته كما يظهر في الأمثلة الآتية:

أنا + مركزي = أنركزية "egocentricism"

حيوان + جرثومة = حيثومة "Sporoza"

تحت + شعور = تحشعوري "subconscious"

كما أنه أثنى على التراكيب المزجية مثل: اللامركزية واللاسلكية، ودعا إلى صوغ مفردات جديدة على نفس القياس مثل:

لا + اخلاق = لا أخلاقي "amoral"

لا + مائي = لا مائي "anhydrous"

لا + أدري = لا أدرية "skepticism"

ولكن الإفراط والتوسع في النحت لم يَرُقْ لكثير من الباحثين والمفكرين. فقد انتقد الشهابي المبالغة في النحت عندما قال عن النحت والمؤيدين له: "إنه أداة صغيرة الأثر إذا قيست بالأدوات السائرة من اشتقاق وتضمين وتعريب، وكأن المتساهلين من أنصار النحت لا يبالون بأن تقضي أراؤهم إلى خلق نبطية جديدة تحل محل اللسان العربي المبين" (551 :1995). كما انتقد الشهابي بعض المصطلحات المنحوتة مثل: خامدرسي)المشتقة من خارج ومدرسة) وتحشعوري (من تحت وشعور)، وفوسوي (من فوق وسوي). ويتساءل: لماذا يخشى هؤلاء استعمال كلمتين عربيتين مقابل كلمة واحدة أعجمية؟.

وقد ساهمت وسائل الإعلام في هذا المجال كثيراً حيث أدخلت العديد من المختصرات التي أصبحت وكأنها كلمات عربية مثل الناتو، واليونسكو، والأليسكو، والأنروا، والأمنستي، والفاو، وناسا، واليونيسيف، والأوبك، والأوابك، والأيدز، وإيكاردا، وفيفا، وأنتربول، ومعاهدة الجات GATT، وإيسيكو، وسانا، وغيرها.

كما شاع استعمال النحت في العصر الحاضر في أسماء الشركات التجارية والمؤسسات والمنظمات الاقتصادية مثل:

جوايكو: الشركة الأردنية للصناعات الخشبية المحدودة "Jordan Wood Industries Company: JWICO"

أدنوك: شركة بترول أبوظبي الوطنية "Abu Dhabi National Oil Company: Adnoc"

دوبال: ألمنيوم دبي "Dubai Aluminum"

سيوى: هيئة كهرباء ومياه الشارقة "Sharjah Electricity and Water Authority: SEWA"

إينوك: شركة نفط الإمارات الوطنية "Emirates National Oil Company: ENOC"

سابتكو: الشركة السعودية للنقل الجماعي "Saudi Public Transport Company: SAPTCO"

يلاحظ أن هذه النحوتات العربية مثل جوايكو وسابتكو قد اشتقت من العبارة الإنجليزية لاسم المؤسسة أو الشركة وليس من الاسم العربي لها، وذلك لصعوبة تكوين كلمة يسهل نطقها من العبارات العربية التي تمثل أسماء كثير من الشركات والمؤسسات.

إن ظاهرة الاختصارات أو ما يسمى بعملية النحت أكثر شيوعاً في اللغة الإنكليزية مما هو عليه الحال في العربية . ومرد ذلك كما يقول حمدان وفارع (2003) إلى أن الكلمات الناتجة بعد النحت أو الاختصار قد تكون ذات معنى غير مناسب وقد يكون النطق بها صعباً نوعاً ما لتجمع أكثر من حرف ساكن في الكلمة المنحوتة. فمثلاً تختصر "حركة التحرير الوطني الفلسطيني" إلى "حتوف" وهي كلمة لا معنى لها ، ثم حذفت منها الواو فأصبحت "حتف"، ووجد أن معنى هذه المنحوتة غير مناسب فعكست كتابة الكلمة فأصبحت "فتح" .ويعزو العباس (2013) عدم شيوع النحت في اللغة العربية إلى النظام الصوتي وبشكل خاص إلى التلفظ بالأبجدية العربية حيث إن الكلمة المنحوتة غالباً ما تتكون من مجموعة من السواكن التي يصعب نطقها دون إضافة أصوات علّة إليها .وفي هذا السياق يقول يعقوب: "وعندنا أن اللغات الأجنبية، وبخاصة المنحدرة من اللغة اللاتينية، أكثر قابلية للنحت من اللغة العربية وأنه في كثير من الأحيان يستحيل في العربية نحت كلمة من كلمتين. ولكن هذا لا يعني أن لغتنا غير قابلة للنحت فإن أحداً لا يستطيع إنكار الكلمات المنحوتة فيها" (212 :1982).

وخلاصة القول: إن النحت وسيلة لإثراء اللغة العربية بالمفردات والمصطلحات الجديدة التي تجعلها قادرة على مواكبة التطور العلمي والتكنولوجي في العصر الحاضر. ولم يعد النحت ترفاً لغوياً بل ضرورة ملحة في ظل التقدم العلمي، لأنه يثري العربية ويعزز مكانتها بين لغات العالم ولكن المبالغة والإفراط في صوغ هذه المنحوتات قد يدفع المتحمسين لها إلى إنتاج مفردات يصعب نطقها ولا يقبلها الذوق اللغوي العام. ولذلك فإن القول بفتح الباب على مصراعيه لعملية النحت يحتاج إلى ضبط وتقييد بحيث لا يؤدي إلى كلمات غريبة منفرة شكلاً ومضموناً. وفي الوقت ذاته لا يحسن بنا أن نغلق هذا الباب ونجعله مقصوراً على المنحوتات القديمة التي شاعت وأصبحت مستساغة، لأن ذلك لا يليق بهذه اللغة حيث إن الحد الشديد من النحت يَصِمُ العربية بالعجز والقصور ويحول دون منافستها للغات الأخرى في التعامل مع تطورات العصر العلمية والتكنولوجية. ومهما يكن الأمر، فإن الذي يحكم على المنحوتات الجديدة بالبقاء أو الاختفاء هو مدى تقبل الناس لها من حيث المعنى واللفظ.

5. التأثير النحوي للترجمة

وهناك جانب آخر لتأثير الترجمة الإعلامية على بنية اللغة العربية وتراكيبها. وأبرز هذه التأثيرات ما درج استعماله في الكتابة الصحفية ونشرات الأخبار المسموعة التي يذكر فيها الضمير العائد قبل ان يُذكر الاسم الذي يعود إليه كما في الأمثلة الآتية:

وفي زيارته غداً للجنوب: هل سيعتذر البشير للجنوبيين عن . . .

يقول السامرائي: "إن الترجمة أثرت على النحو في اللغة العربية، فقد تأثرت الجملة العربية في بنائها وترتيب الكلمات والعبارات فيها بالأساليب الغربية كما في المثال الآتي: والمسألة، بالرغم من أنها ليست بذات قيمة، فإنها تؤثر في . . . والأصل أن يقال: والمسألة تؤثر في . . . بالرغم من أنها . . ." (8 :1997).

وهناك ميل متزايد لدى المترجمين والكتاب العرب لاستعمال صيغ مثل "أكثر وضوحاً" "more apparent" و "أكثر دقة" "more exact" و "أكثر اتساعا" "more extensive" بدلاً من "أوضح" و "أدق"

و "أوسع" على التوالي كما ذكر محمد عصفور (205 :2007). وهناك توجه لاستعمال كاف التشبيه في عبارات لا تمت للتشبيه بصلة مثل "الواقعية كمفهوم أدبي" و "البرلمان كسلطة تشريعية" (عصفور، 205 :2007).

كما أن ترجمة الظرف باللغة الإنجليزية إلى اللغة العربية يجانب المألوف في الأسلوب العربي حيث تضاف كلمة "بشكل" أو "بطريقة" أو "على نحو" إلى الظرف كما في:

بشكل طبيعي (طبيعياً) "naturally"
بشكل واسع (بتوسع، بشدة) "extensively"
بطريقة حكيمة (بحكمة) "wisely"

6. أثر الترجمة الدلالي

أدت الترجمة إلى توسيع مدلولات بعض المفردات بحيث أصبحت تشير إلى معانٍ جديدة لم تكن سابقاً جزءاً منها كما في كلمة "سقف" التي كانت تطلق على غطاء المنزل وهو أعلاه المقابلُ للأرض (المعجم الوسيط). أما اليوم فيقال في الأوساط الأكاديمية "رفع رئيس القسم سقف المادة" (زاد عدد الطلبة فيها)، ويقال "ارتفع سقف مطالب المحتجين". وكلمة "أثاث" التي كانت تعني "متاع البيت، من فراش ونحوه" والأثاث "المالُ أجمعُ من ماشية وغيرها" (25 :1972) المعجم الوسيط. أما اليوم فقد اقتصر معناها على متاع البيت من فراش ونحوه. ويمكن اعتبار هذا النوع من التغير الدلالي تضييقاً لمدلولات الكلمة. ومن قبيل التوسع الدلالي ما حدث لكلمة "احتجّ" التي كانت تعني "يقدم حجة"، أما في لغة العصر فقد اتسع معناها ليصبح "استنكر" أو "اعترض" كما في الجملة "احتجّت الحكومة على الاعتداءات المتكررة". ويقول السامرائي في كتابه التطور اللغوي التاريخي: "إن كلمة "شجب" تعني أصلاً "حَزِن أو هَلك"، أما في لغة اليوم فقد أصبحت تعني "ندّد واستنكر" (129 :1997).

ويتضمن التوسع الدلالي أيضاً استعارة بعض الصفات التي لا تستخدم في العربية إلا لوصف الإنسان، واستخدامها لوصف كلمات لم تكن توصف بها سابقاً كما في الأمثلة الآتية:

"فكرة جريئة" و "مشروع شجاع" و "ميزانية متواضعة" و "معاهدة ظالمة" و "سياسة رشيدة" و "مدينة فاضلة" و "ملاحظة خجولة"، وغيرها.

يقول السامرائي: "إن كل هذه الأوصاف تطلق على الإنسان، ولكنها أصبحت تلصق مجازاً في مفردات لم تكن تلتصق بها سابقاً" (7 :1997). ونلاحظ هنا أن للترجمة الإعلامية تأثيرات إيجابية في معظمها، ولكن التأثيرات السلبية تعزى إلى نقص في كفاءة المترجم الذي لا يدرك أنه من الممكن صياغة هذه التراكيب صياغة أخرى وفقاً للمقبول في الأسلوب العربي.

7. التأثير المجازي للترجمة على اللغة العربية

يُعد استعمال العبارات المجازية من تشبيه وتشخيص ومبالغة وكناية وتورية واستعارة أمراً شائعاً بين الناطقين بلغة ما. ولم تعد العبارات المجازية مجرد ترف لغوي تزخر به الفنون الأدبية كالشعر والرواية فحسب، بل أصبح شائعاً جداً في لغتنا اليومية في المجالات الصحفية والاقتصادية والعلمية أحياناً. وهناك عبارات مجازية جديدة تتسرب إلى اللغة عن طريق الترجمة وبخاصة عندما لا يوجد في اللغة المقترِضة عبارة ثابتة تعبر عن العبارة الأجنبية كما في الأمثلة الآتية:

"الخط الأحمر"، و "الكرة في ملعب . . ."، و "أوراق الضغط"، و "تحت الطاولة"، و "كشف أوراقه . . ."، و "التعتيم الإعلامي"، و "التغطية الإعلامية"، و "الخط الساخن"، و "الضوء الأخضر"، و "هجرة الدماغ"،

و "ضربة استباقية" و "حرب خاطفة"، و "سياسة الأرض المحروقة"، و "سجل هدفاً"، و "الكرة في مرمى . . ."، و "الستار الحديدي"، و "رياح التغيير"، و "وصلت المفاوضات إلى طريق مسدود"، و "خلف الكواليس"، و "قفزة في الظلام"، و "رهان خاسر"، وغيرها.

ومن العبارات الاصطلاحية التي دخلت إلى العربية عن طريق الترجمة ما ذكره أبو السيدة (113 :2004) مثل:

نهاية الطريق	"the end of the road"
لاح في الأفق	"loomed in the horizon"
آفاق أرحب	"wider horizons"
كوّن صورة	"formed a picture"

تدل هذه العبارات وغيرها إلى أن الترجمة أدت إلى إثراء اللغة العربية بعبارات مجازية وعبارات اصطلاحية في ميادين شتى كالسياسة والاقتصاد والرياضة والإعلام والعلوم العسكرية.

الخلاصة

يستطيع المرء بكل ثقة أن يخلص إلى القول إن اللغة العربية لغة حية قادرة على التطور والتغير تطوراً يمكّنها من استيعاب التحديات الاصطلاحية والعلمية والتكنولوجية لتنفي عن نفسها تهمة العجز والقصور. ولا بد لنا أن نتذكر دائماً أن العربية في جميع مراحل تطورها لم تكن يوماً في معزل عن غيرها من اللغات، ولن تكون كذلك، فهي تؤثر في غيرها وتتأثر بها أيضاً. وفي هذا السياق يقول حسان: "و . . . ما تجربه اللغة العربية الآن من تعرض لنفوذ اللغات الأجنبية لا يستحق كل هذا الجزع من جانب أحبار اللغة، لأنه ظاهرة اجتماعية لغوية جربتها العربية في الجاهلية والإسلام، ولا تزال تجربها حتى اليوم" (117 :2001). ويضيف السامرائي: "إن من الواجب علينا أن نفسح لهذا الجديد الذي قذف به المستعملون مكاناً في كتبنا اللغوية لأنه صار من مادة هذه اللغة" (376 :1997).

إن انفتاح اللغة العربية على الثقافات الأخرى والتفاعل معها والتأثر بها والتأثير عليها يجعلها لغة معاصرة، قادرة على المنافسة ومواكبة التحديات اللغوية والعلمية بأساليب واستراتيجيات متنوعة. ولعل الترجمة من اللغات الأخرى إلى العربية كانت وما تزال من أهم استراتيجيات تطوير اللغة وأكبر مصادر إثرائها وتحسين قدرتها على المعاصرة والمنافسة واستيعاب ما يستجد من ألفاظ واصطلاحات علمية وتكنولوجية واقتصادية وسياسية. وبالرغم من بعض التأثيرات السلبية للترجمة على اللغة العربية في النواحي الاشتقاقية والتركيبية والأسلوبية، تظل الترجمة، دون منازع، أوسع مصدر وأكثر وسيلة لإغناء اللغة العربية بالكثير من المفردات والتعابير المجازية، ولكن يجب ألا يُترك باب الترجمة والتعريب مفتوحاً على مصراعيه، إذ لا بد من ضوابط معينة لعملية التعريب والاشتقاق من المنحوتات ذات الأصل الأجنبي.

وتنبغي الإشارة إلى ضرورة كون هذه المنحوتات مختصرة حتى يسهل لفظها ويشيع تداولها بين الناس. وعلاوة على ذلك يحسن أن تنسجم المنحوتات الجديدة مع قواعد الصياغة والاشتقاق ما استطعنا إلى ذلك سبيلا. لقد مرت اللغة العربية في مراحل كثيرة من التطور من العصر الجاهلي إلى عصر صدر الإسلام ثم إلى العهد العباسي وأخيراً اللغة العربية المعاصرة المستخدمة هذه الأيام. وطرأت عليها تغيرات وتطورات عديدة في هذه المراحل المختلفة بحيث يستطيع الدارس تمييز خصائص لغوية محددة للغة العربية في كل مرحلة.

يقول حسان: "وإنا لنجد هذا التوسع في التعريب والترجمة والصوغ القياسي يسود الاستعمال اللغوي في أيامنا هذه مع اختلاف في المادة التي يجري تعريبها أو ترجمتها أو صوغها ارتجالياً عما كانت عليه في العصر العباسي" (183 :2001).

لقد أصبحت الترجمة أمراً واقعاً واستراتيجية لا يستغنى عنها للإرتقاء باللغة العربية وإثرائها بالنتاج الفكري والعلمي والتكنولوجي للشعوب الأخرى. ولذلك يقول ذو الغنى (2011) في استعراض له لكتاب العلامة ف. عبد الرحيم بعنوان معجم الدخيل: "إن المفردات الأجنبية الدخيلة ظاهرة طبيعية وعامة في معظم اللغات وهي من عوامل إثراء اللغات في مفرداتها. وإن نقاء اللغة—أي لغة—من شوائب الدخيل دليل على فقرها . . ." (1 :2011).

لقد اتضح مما سبق أن الترجمة تلعب دوراً كبيراً في اثراء اللغة العربية و بخاصة في مجال المفردات والمصطلحات. وهذا ما يفسر دخول العديد من المفردات و العبارات إلى اللغة العربية و شيوعها إلى الحد الذي لم نعد نشعر فيه أنها مفردات لم تكن أصلاً موجودة في اللغة العربية. و في ضوء النتائج التي أظهرتها الدراسة فإن الترجمة وسيلة فعالة لإثراء العربية وتطويرها. ويحسن لنا في الختام أن نقترح التوصيات الآتية.

1. تفعيل دور الترجمة من اللغات الأخرى إلى اللغة العربية لتزويدها بالنتاج الفكري والعلمي والتكنولوجي والمعرفي عامة، وذلك بإنشاء مؤسسات خاصة بالترجمة على مستوى كل دولة لاختيار الكتب النافعة للأمة ونقلها إلى العربية
2. إنشاء مراكز خاصة بالترجمة في الجامعات العربية يشارك فيها مختصون في الترجمة وفي اللغة العربية
3. زيادة التعاون بين مجامع اللغة العربية في الوطن العربي في مجال توحيد المصطلحات المترجمة بدلاً من ترجمتها بأشكال مختلفة في كل دولة
4. إصدار معجم خاص بالمصطلحات الجديدة المترجمة والمعربة بشكل دوري يشتمل على ما استجد من مصطلحات مترجمة، الأمر الذي ينشر هذه المصطلحات ويعمل على توحيد استعمالها بين المترجمين في أرجاء الوطن العربي كافة، ومن الممكن أيضاً تحميل هذه المعاجم إلكترونياً في مواقع محددة ليسهل استعمالها وينتشر بسرعة
5. ينبغي لكل مؤسسة تعنى بالترجمة أن تعين مدققاً لغوياً أو محرراً صحفياً لمراجعة كل ما يترجم والتأكد من سلامته لغوياً تفادياً لكثير من الأخطاء اللغوية في المواد المترجمة سواء أكانت كتباً أم كتابات صحفية
6. تقنين مهنة الترجمة بحيث لا يُسمح إلا للأكفاء في هذا الميدان بممارسة الترجمة
7. الإفادة من أساليب تدريس اللغة الإنجليزية في تدريس مواد اللغة العربية وبخاصة في مجال تعليم الكتابة والوظائف اللغوية، ولا سيما أن ميدان أساليب تدريس اللغة الإنجليزية قد تطور تطوراً هائلاً، فلا ضير في ترجمة هذه الأساليب والإفادة منها قدر المستطاع في تدريس مهارات اللغة العربية وبخاصة تدريس اللغة العربية لغير الناطقين بها .وفي هذا المجال يقول الكاتب الحمّار في مقالة له بعنوان "التعريب العكسي :رؤية عربية مع الاستئناس بالأجنبية" :"ولعل أكبر عائق أمام العربية يبرز عندما نراقبها وهي تُدَرس" (2 :2011). ويقترح الإفادة من طرق تدريس اللغة الأجنبية في تدريس العربية بتدريس مادة تسمى "درس اللغة المقارن"
8. تعزيز تدريس اللغة العربية في برامج إعداد المترجمين على جميع المستويات وبخاصة في مجالات النحو والصرف والأسلوب.

وأخيراً لا بد لنا أن ندرك أن اللغة ظاهرة إنسانية حية تخضع، شأنها في ذلك شأن سائر جوانب السلوك الإنساني، إلى عوامل التغيير زماناً ومكاناً سلباً وإيجاباً. وإن التطور اللغوي أمر حتمي، وبخاصة التطور الناجم عن تأثير الترجمة في مختلف الجوانب اللغوية. كما أن آثار هذا التغير إيجابية في معظمها ولكنها لا تخلو من سلبيات يمكن تداركها والحد منها.

المراجع باللغة العربية

البعلبكي، منير. 2000. المورد: قاموس إنكليزي عربي. بيروت:دار العلم للملايين.

الجبر، خالد عبد الرؤوف. 2009. اللغة العربية في الصحف اليومية والأسبوعية. عمان: مجمع اللغة العربية الأردني.

حسان، تمام. 2001. اللغة بين المعيارية والوصفية. القاهرة: عالم الكتب.

الحصري، ساطع. 1985. في اللغة والأدب وعلاقتهما بالقومية. بيروت: مركز دراسات الوحدة العربية.

الحمّار، محمد مصطفى. 2011. التعريب العكسي: رؤية عربية مع الاستئناس بالأجنبية—توصيات المؤتمر السنوي السادس عشر لتعريب العلوم بالقاهرة. القاهرة: الجمعية المصرية لتعريب العلوم.

ذو الغنى، أيمن بن أحمد. 2011. العلامة ف. عبدالرحيم وكتابه معجم الدخيل (http://www.odabasham.net).

السامرائي، إبراهيم .1997. العربية تاريخ وتطور. بيروت: مكتبة المعارف.

الشهابي، مصطفى. 1995. المصطلحات العلمية في اللغة العربية في القديم والحديث. بيروت: دار صادر.

العباس، عبدالحي. 2013. عن النحت في العربية المعاصرة. (http://www.angelfire.com/tx4/lisan/lex-zam/dilalahessays/naht2.htm).

عصفور، محمد. 2007. تأثير الترجمة على اللغة العربية. مجلة جامعة الشارقة للعلوم الشرعية والإنسانية 4(2): 195–216.

قاموس أطلس الموسوعي: إنكليزي- عربي. 2003. القاهرة:أطلس للنشر.

مجمع اللغة العربية. 1972. المعجم الوسيط. أستانبول: دار الدعوة.

يعقوب، أميل بديع. 1982. فقه اللغة العربية وخصائصها. بيروت: دار العلم للملايين.

References

Abu Al-Sayyidah, Abdul Fattah. 2004. "Translation of Idioms into Arabic." *Babel* 50, no. 2: 114–31.

Al-Abbas, Abdul Ḥayy. 2013. "al-Naḥt fī al-Lugha al-ʿArabiyya al-Muʿāṣira." April 18. http://www.angelfire.com/tx4/lisan/lex_zam/dilalahessays/naht2.htm.

Al-Baalabki, Munir. 2000. *al-Mawrid: English-Arabic Dictionary*. Beirut: Dār al-ʿIlm li-l-Malāyīn.

Al-Hammār, Muhammad Mustafa. 2011. *al-Taʿrīb al-ʿAksī: Ruʾyah ʿArabiyya maʿa al-ʾIstiʾnās bil-ʾAjnabiyya—Tawṣiyāt al-Muʾtamar al-Sanawiyy al-Sādis ʿAshar li-Taʿrīb al-ʿUlūm bil-Qāhira*. Cairo: Egypt: Al-Jamʿiyya al-Miṣriyya li-Taʿrīb al-ʿUlūm.

Al-Huṣarī, Saṭiʿ. 1985. *fī al-Lugha wa al-ʾAdab wa ʿAlāqatihimā bil-Qawmiyya*. Beirut, Lebanon: Markiz Dirāsāt al-Wahda al-ʿArabiyya.

Ali, Abdul Sahib M. 2005. "Calquing: A Means of Terminological Enrichment." *Turjuman* 14, no. 1: 113–35.

Al-Jabr, Khalid Abdul Raouf. 2009. *al-Lugha al-'Arabiyya fī al-Ṣuḥuf al-Yawmiyya wa al-Usbū'iyya*. Amman, Jordan: Majma' al-Lughah al-'Arabiyya al-'Urdunī.

Al-Samurrā'ī, Ibrahim. 1997. *al-'Arabiyya Tārīkh wa Taṭawwur*. Beirut: Maktabat al-Ma'ārif.

Al-Shihābī, Mustafā. 1995. *al-Muṣṭalaḥāt al-'Ilmiyya fī al-Lugha al-'Arabiyya fī al-Qadīm wa al-Ḥadīth*. Beirut: Dār Ṣādir.

Arlotto, Anthony. 1972. *Introduction to Historical Linguistics*. New York: University Press of America.

Bynon, Theodora. 1997. *Historical Linguistics*. Cambridge: Cambridge University Press.

Elmggrab, Ramadan Ahmed. 2011. "Methods of Creating and Introducing New Terms in Arabic: Contributions from English-Arabic Translation." *IPEDR* 26: 491–500.

Hamdan, Jihad, and Shehdeh Fareh. 2003. "Acronyms in English and Arabic." *Dirasat: Human and Social Sciences* 30, no. 1: 183–93.

Hassan, Tammam. 2001. *al-Lugha bayna al-Mi'yāriyya wa al-Waṣfiyya*. Cairo: 'Ālam al-Kutub.

Hudson, Grover. 2000. *Essential Introductory Linguistics*. Oxford: Blackwell.

Ibrahim, Zeinab. 2006. "Borrowing in Modern Standard Arabic." Accessed November 16, 2016, http://www.inst.at/trans/16Nr/01_4/zeinab16.htm.

Majma' Al-Lugha Al-'Arabiyya. 1972. *al-Mu'jam al-Wasīṭ*. Istanbul: Dār al-Da'wa.

Qāmūs Aṭlas al-Mawsū'ī: English–Arabic. 2003. Cairo: Aṭlas lil-Nashr.

Thul-Ghina, Ayman bin Ahmad. 2011. "al-'Allāma F. Abdul Rahīm wa Kitābuh *Mu'jam al-Dakhīl*." April 18. http://www.odabasham.net.

'Usfūr, Muhammad. 2007. "Ta'thīr al-Tarjamah 'alā al-Lugha al-'Arabiyya." *Majallat Jāmi'at al-Shāriqa lil-'Ulūm al-Shar'iyya wa al-'Insāniyya* 4, no. 2: 195–216.

Ya'qūb, Emil Badī'. 1982. *Fiqh al-Lugha al-'Arabiyya wa Khaṣā'iṣuh*. Beirut: Dār al-'Ilm li-l-Malāyīn.

REVIEW

Perspectives on Arabic Linguistics XXVIII: Papers from the Annual Symposium on Arabic Linguistics, Gainesville, Florida, 2014

Youssef A. Haddad and Eric Potsdam, eds.

Amsterdam: John Benjamins, 2016. xii + 248 pp., index. ISBN: 9789027200327. Hardcover, $188.00.

Reviewed by Uri Horesh, University of Essex

The *Perspectives* subseries of the Benjamins series Studies in Arabic Linguistics (this is volume 4 of the Studies series) needs little introduction to scholars of Arabic linguistics. It is a long-standing, quasi-annual publication, of which the current volume is the twenty-seventh, the numbering having begun in the series' previous iteration, often referred to informally as "the pink series" because of the color of the book cover prior to the Studies era. This particular volume includes ten articles based on presentations at the 2014 annual symposium organized by the Arabic Linguistics Society and held at the University of Florida. These articles are classified within three parts: phonetics and phonology, syntax, and sociolinguistics.

Normally, in a review of an edited volume, one begins with a chapter-by-chapter description of the contents. However, the editors—as editors often do—have done this for us in their concise introduction to the volume (pp. ix–xii). In this introduction, I was happy to read that the volume "draws attention to the micro-variation that exists among" Arabic dialects (ix). Micro-variation as a concept has mostly been applied to the kind of work done by variationist sociolinguists. Yet, while this volume only includes one paper classified as sociolinguistics, the majority of the other papers do indeed use data from one or more varieties of Arabic (and related languages; more on that below) to illustrate variations through the prisms of different theoretical frameworks—or "perspectives," as the title prescribes. In the remainder of this review, then, I focus on the contribution of the volume as a whole to the study of Arabic linguistics and the variation found and explained therein, with references to specific papers when warranted.

Unlike some previous volumes of *Perspectives*, many of which could be considered similar to a journal issue, in which most articles are not related to one another, I felt as if the papers in this volume do in fact form a somewhat cohesive collection of thoughts and ideas. Surely, as the papers are highly professional and include jargon and technical notations (e.g., statistical analysis, syntactic trees, spectrograms), they also present data in a way that is accessible to readers who specialize in subfields of linguistics other than the authors'. Take, for example, the first paper by Janet Watson and Barry Heselwood. This paper is based on Watson's keynote address at the Florida conference but adds to it fine-grained phonetic analysis while articulately introducing readers not only to a variety of Arabic (San'ani) but also to neighboring Modern South Arabian languages. While the latter are by no means varieties of Arabic, they form part of the Semitic phylum of which Arabic is a significant member. Moreover, they overlap territorially with Arabic varieties of the southern Arabian Peninsula. For many scholars of Arabic, these general facts are well known, but Watson and Heselwood spell out in detail how varieties of these two branches of Semitic interact.

The volume represents a wide range of Arabic dialects. In Cheng-Wei Lin's paper alone, there is a survey of twenty varieties (one of them is Modern Standard Arabic) and a novel application of Nick Clements's Feature Economy framework. Other papers include Palestinian dialects from both the Galilee (Dua'a Abu Elhija Mahajna and Stuart Davis) and Gaza (William Cotter), Jordanian (Zafer Lababidi and Hanyong Park; Ahmad Alqassas), and other dialects such as Moroccan and Egyptian varieties, scattered throughout the volume. It is particularly pleasing to see under-studied dialects prominently represented in the volume. Notably, Faruk Akkuş, in a solo paper and one coauthored with Elabbas Benmamoun, analyzes aspects of the syntax of the Anatolian Sason dialect, and Cotter presents a quantitative sociolinguistic analysis of Gaza City Arabic.

Language contact is dealt with in a number of papers. Lababidi and Park present experimental evidence pertaining to Arabic–English contact among different combinations of L1/L2 speakers of either language. Interestingly, this paper is included in the part of the book devoted to phonetics and phonology. Cotter makes reference to dialect contact within Gaza between original inhabitants of the city and refugees from Jaffa in central Palestine. Akkuş and Benmamoun's paper takes into consideration contact between the Sason dialect (in southeastern Turkey) and Mesopotamian dialects (e.g., the Iraqi dialect of Mosul).

Finally, a few words about the organization of the volume and its significance. As alluded to in the previous paragraph, I find the inclusion of a second language acquisition (SLA) paper in the same section of the book as other papers in phonetics and phonology a bit peculiar. I understand that, had there been an SLA section, this would have been the only paper in it, but Cotter's sociolinguistics paper is also a lone wolf in its section—and it, too, deals with a phonological variable. Perhaps the editors could have simply divided the volume into phonetics and phonology in one section (and included the paper in sociolinguistics) and syntax in the other. But this is a minor point. The book itself is well packaged, neatly printed, and easy to read. It is unfortunate that the price is prohibitive for the average scholar, let alone student; this applies to the ebook edition as well, which is priced just as high as the hardbound book.

In today's age of fierce competition in academia and the demand to publish in "leading journals," one needs to think what the benefits are in publishing a paper in a volume like *Perspectives* versus a conventional periodical journal. Yes, *Perspectives* volumes are all peer reviewed (I can attest to that as a reviewer for the series myself, though not for this volume), but some universities and other institutions—especially, it seems, in the English-speaking world—frown upon edited volumes, usually with no good reason. This volume, as many of its predecessors, comprises papers that could easily have made it into reputable journals in their respective subfields of linguistics. It is a pity that metrics like "impact factor" are used as a proxy for "quality."

REVIEW

Case Endings in Spoken Standard Arabic: Statistics, Norms, and Diversity in Unscripted Formal Speech

Andreas Hallberg.

Studia Orientalia Lundensia, nova series no. 4. Lund, Sweden: Lund University, 2016. xiii + 260 pp., appendices, bibliography, general index, author index. ISBN: 9789187833694. http://www.ht.lu.se/en/series/sol/.

Reviewed by Paul A. Sundberg, Director, Gulf Arabic Program, Sultanate of Oman

Andreas Hallberg's dissertation exploring the norms of Spoken Standard Arabic (SSA) fills a critical need in the literature for empirical studies on the actual use of *iʿrāb* by "proficient, highly educated native speakers of Arabic" when speaking Standard Arabic extemporaneously in formal situations (6). Indeed, it has implications in three areas: (a) for language instruction (his primary motivation) to inform curriculum development and formulate authentic proficiency goals, (b) for language reform in the Arab world to address the conservative language ideology in national Arabic curricula, and (c) for linguistic theory, especially diglossic variation.

The study was motivated by a desire for a model of authentic case usage to implement in the classroom and the lack of detailed descriptions of this register in the literature. The only "model" available has been that of the traditional grammarians: full inflection of every noun not in pausal position, guidelines that correspond little with how Modern Standard Arabic is actually spoken.

As his corpus, Hallberg selected seventeen interviews from Al-Jazeera's program *Liqā' al-Yawm* with Arab opinion makers such as Muḥammad al-Barādiʿī and Ṣā'ib 'Arīqāt. He then created a "disambiguated dataset" of nearly fifteen thousand noun and adjective tokens, after first excluding various categories of nouns (e.g., names, numbers above ten, nouns in formulaic expressions). Morphosyntactic codes were then added to each token (especially whether case-marked or -unmarked) for computer analysis.

Results showed roughly 70 percent of noun tokens were unmarked, with only about 10 percent marked for case. (Remaining percentages were tokens ambiguously marked for case, grammatically indeclinable, or with inaudible endings.) Only 0.3 percent of tokens had case errors, implying that "speakers only insert case endings when they are certain that they can do so correctly" (165).

One of the most striking findings was the wide variation in case use among speakers, ranging from 0.2 percent of potential case endings used (Munīb al-Miṣrī) to an outlier high of 42.2 percent (Ṭayyib Tīzīnī). The second-highest user was Muḥammad Badīʿ, at 18.3 percent. Most subjects' case use ranged from 1.5 percent to 5 percent. Speakers also maintained a consistent rate of case marking throughout their interviews, whether low or high, confounding a common assumption of "discourse drift" (i.e., speakers starting with a show of case use, then moving to a more informal style). The data revealed two distinct groups of SSA speakers by their case marking behavior: those with high overall case marking and those with mid and low case marking. Idiosyncratic variation was even seen in speakers' preferences for which structures and contexts to assign marked case.

As for morphological effects on case use, the study presents quantitative findings for various noun paradigms, degrees of definiteness, and four specific nominal types. Of the eight noun paradigms, the three most frequent were the triptote paradigm of nouns with three distinctive case vowels (86 percent of tokens in the dataset but only a 4.1 percent likelihood of being marked), sound feminine plurals (5.5 percent of the dataset, with a 2.7 percent likelihood), and diptotes (3.8 percent of the tokens; likelihood 2 percent). Although less frequent, the dual and sound masculine plural paradigms were "by far the most favored for case marking" in nominative position (-ān/-ūn) than any other paradigm: a 42.4 percent likelihood (205). However, only four speakers consistently made this distinction, with the others using the "unmarked" (dialectical) option of -ayn/-īn in all contexts.

Importantly, in terms of the four types of *definiteness,* case marking was shown to be hierarchical, with this hierarchy consistent across speakers. A key finding was that nouns with a definite article are almost never marked for case (0.3 percent likelihood), regardless of speaker. Slightly more likely (2.8 percent) was case on nouns in construct state (i.e., the *muḍāf),* indefinite nouns (5.3 percent), and, strikingly, nouns with an attached pronoun (43.9 percent). However, case before *-hu,* the most frequent attached pronoun, was consistently distinguished by only two speakers; the others reduced this three-way distinction to one "unmarked" (but standard) form

-u(h) in most contexts. (Hallberg selected speakers of Egyptian and Levantine dialects only.)

Other morphological phenomena examined were the indefinite accusative marked orthographically by *alif* (e.g., *bayt-an*) and nouns with *tā' marbūṭa*. These two, like duals and sound masculine plurals, give evidence for the "strong effect of orthographic case marking on speech" (217), with 41.2 percent of nouns written with final *alif* marked by spoken case also, whereas only 0.6 percent of words ending in *tā' marbūṭa* were marked in speech.

In his final chapter, Hallberg describes how syntactic features interact with case in SSA. Head nouns were found to be marked for case five times more (2.7 percent likelihood) than their following attributive adjectives (0.6 percent). As for the three cases themselves, marking rates differed: accusative case was marked three times more (9.7 percent) than nominative or genitive cases (3.0 percent and 2.6 percent, respectively), proportions true for every subject in the study. To explain this, Hallberg points out the evident orthographic effects of final *alif,* used both to mark the object of a verb (8 percent) and the complement of *kāna* and her sisters (15 percent). Finally, the correlation between case marking and core syntactic roles (e.g., subject and object) appears not to be governed by covert linguistic norms but appears highly idiosyncratic, each speaker favoring different syntactic roles for case over others, with a general tendency to favor accusative positions such as verbal object and complement of *kāna.*

As for the study's pedagogical implications, Hallberg concludes that the spoken patterns he observed suggest a number of "covert linguistic norms" governing the use of case that differ from traditional norms, entailing "partial abandonment of the prescriptive ideal" in teaching Arabic as a foreign language (255). Instead, a curriculum is needed that helps learners achieve oral proficiency in authentic SSA. In this register of Modern Standard Arabic, the noun/adjective unmarked for case is the default; hence, case marking should be taught largely as "an optional addition" (not an optional dropping) since the average proficient native-speaker adds case only 7 percent of the time. Another implication is that the case system is better introduced "relatively late," mainly as passive knowledge. Finally, students should be taught for authenticity to potentially mark certain categories of nouns/adjectives for case in their speech and not to mark others based on the covert norms described above.

REVIEW

Ahlan wa Sahlan: Functional Modern Standard Arabic for Beginners, 2nd ed.

Mahdi Alosh, revised with Allen Clark.

New Haven, CT: Yale University Press, 2010. xxiv + 668 pp., appendices, glossary, indices. ISBN: 9780300219890. Hardcover, $78.00.

Reviewed by Yahya Kharrat, Western University, London, Ontario, Canada

Institutions of higher learning in Europe and America are preparing themselves to teach Arabic by engaging a large number of specialized teachers formulating curricula for its study. These curricula rest upon well-established principles for the acquisition of languages and rely on a rich field of practical pedagogy. *Ahlan wa Sahlan: Functional Modern Standard Arabic for Beginners,* 2nd edition, by Mahdi Alosh, is a recent addition to these curricula and a fine contribution to this field of education, whose aim is to teach Arabic to the nonnative speaker. Its goal is to assist the student by providing exercises that focus on the four principal proficiencies of language acquisition: listening, speaking, reading, and writing.

The book is divided into twenty-four chapters. Each chapter begins by showcasing, through a casual dialogue, a particular aspect of Arabic culture. The author introduces in well-expressed language the vocabulary that the student needs in his or her daily life, whether at home, at university, at work, or through various social relationships. Each chapter ends with exercises and simplified grammatical rules that help the student interact with the text of the lesson and develop linguistic skills. The audio, video, and online interactive exercises included with the book contain the vocalized lessons designed to generate discussion along with questions to be answered by listening to the recited text of the lesson. A new version of this book was published by Yale in 2015 with "online media," which gives students access to a website containing all the material formerly on an included CD and DVD.

The Arabic text in the initial lessons is quite limited, whereas the English text is extensive. The second half of the book reverses the pattern and presents us with a large amount of Arabic text. It would be preferable for the proportion of Arabic to English to increase gradually, following the progression of the student working his or her way through the lessons.

The grammatical rules along with supporting exercises provided by this book help the student practice the lessons during the early stages of instruction, facilitating a familiarity with grammatical terms such as the definite and indefinite articles, the sun and moon letters, verbs, subjects and objects, and adjectives with their modified nouns. It also introduces nominal sentences with their subject and predicate and the correct use of cardinal and ordinal numbers. The three syntactical cases are introduced—the nominative, accusative, and genitive—along with the singular, dual, and plural. Although the author introduces these grammatical rules, the text does not provide a sufficient number of practice exercises to allow the student to truly master them. All the exercises follow the same pattern throughout the book, which risks making the practical work seem tedious and repetitive. Hopefully, future editions of the book will address this problem and enliven the student's interaction with the text by adding some variety and creativity.

The author gives each of the chapters an Arabic title to provide a theme for each lesson, and the beginning of each chapter sets forth the chapter's objectives. A vocabulary of new words for the lesson is placed at the end of the chapter to facilitate the student's work. At the end of each lesson, we find a discussion using its didactic content along with corresponding questions and exercises, providing the student with a deeper understanding of the text and enabling the acquisition of some basic conversational skills. The author also includes exercises that help the student acquire a vocabulary of synonyms and antonyms. In these exercises, the student is presented with a group of words and asked to underline the word that is inappropriate. Another exercise presents two columns of words and invites the student to provide a middle column by matching the meaning of these words. Both of these methods enrich the student's learning experience. The author further stimulates the student's intellect by requiring him or her to rearrange a group of random words to form a meaningful sentence. In addition to this, in a similar task, the student is required to rearrange a group of seemingly unrelated but complete sentences into a meaningful, coherent, and complete paragraph. Not only does this give the student an example of correct sentence structure, but it also serves to engage the student's ability to connect sentences with a related theme into a comprehensible paragraph. The student is also encouraged to develop conversational skills by interacting with fellow classmates while discussing the topics presented by the recorded narrative.

At the end of each lesson the author includes a list of the verbs used in the accompanying narrative along with their conjugations in the past and present tenses and in the imperative mood. These conjugations assist the student to develop an understanding that facilitates the application of the rules to other verbs not mentioned in the text. Furthermore, the major verbs mentioned throughout the book are also listed at the end of the book in appendix C (p. 550). The answers to all the exercises and questions are found in appendix D (p. 564). A complete vocabulary in alphabetical order is found on page 615.

A suggestion I would make to the author is to leave the study of the hamza and the rules governing the placement of the glottal stop out of this beginner's book and make it part of the book at the intermediate level. The complexity of the rules and the exceptions to these rules make this subject a challenge even for advanced readers, let alone those at the beginner's level. The text as it stands presents us with some examples of these difficulties. For instance, on line 5 of page 118, the middle hamza of *yaqra'ūn* ("they read") is written with the hamza on the alif whereas, according to rules of precedence, the proper spelling would have the hamza written on the waw. Similarly, on page 536, on the fifth line from the bottom, the word *yasū'ukum* should be written with the hamza on the line rather than on the waw. Attention should also be paid to the proper use of the initial hamza at the beginning of the word *al-ithnayn* ("Monday," 202): this is an elided glottal stop and must be deleted.

In conclusion, it is hoped that this brief review will provide the author with an opportunity to address some issues that may help improve the forthcoming edition, making it even more beneficial for universities in Europe and America and for all those who strive to achieve a level of proficiency in the Arabic language. This useful work can be recommended in the field of teaching Arabic as a foreign language.

REVIEW

Ahlan wa Sahlan: Functional Modern Standard Arabic for Intermediate Learners, 2nd ed.

Mahdi Alosh, revised with Allen Clark.

New Haven, CT: Yale University Press, 2013. vii + 677 pp., glossary, appendix, index.
ISBN: 9780300178777. Hardcover, $85.00.

Reviewed by Janelle Moser, University of Arizona

The second edition of *Ahlan wa Sahlan* provides a compelling follow-up to the book for novice-level learners of the same series. Designed to cover approximately 150 instructional hours, the textbook sticks to the "functional approach" to teaching and learning Modern Standard Arabic (MSA)—that is, "performing language functions and using them in contexts that simulate reality" (xxi). The realistic, goal-oriented approach to learning outcomes provides content in line with the ACTFL Proficiency Guidelines, which require intermediate-high language users to understand "short, non-complex texts that convey basic information and deal with personal and social topics" as well as the general intermediate-level dictum to "understand texts that convey basic information such as that found in announcements, notices, and online bulletin boards and forums" (Swender, Conrad, and Vicars 2012). The lessons are structured by first introducing lesson-level learning objectives, highlighting outcomes related to grammar and those revisited from previous lessons. The clear outlining of these learning objectives will be appreciated by instructors and students alike. Moreover, highly functional genres such as signs and advertisements, recipes, and interviews are introduced early and often. The inclusion of these genres based on chapter themes fits well with current trends in the second language acquisition literature supporting the introduction of simple genres as a means for eventually scaffolding awareness of conventional textual features onto more complex texts (Azaz 2016; Byrnes et al. 2006; Hyland 2007).

A review of selected learning objectives and grammatical points covered shows a great deal of engaging topics and themes with a high level of utility for learners. Lesson 1 provides an introduction to announcements and advertisements in Arabic and introduces conditional sentences with إذا, defective nouns (الاسم المنقوص), and noun structure (اسم الفعل). Lesson 3 covers learning how to follow written recipes and how to describe food as well as giving and receiving instructions and expressing obligation with يجب, uses of the preposition bi-, and adverbial use of ordinal numbers. Lesson 9 covers learning to describe vacations and places of interest and introduces historical personalities and events through narration. Prepositional phrases and verb–preposition collocational phrases are also introduced. Later chapters begin introducing more abstract genres and themes, with Lesson 19 introducing proverbs, their history, and contexts as well as idiomatic expressions. The thoughtfully chosen assortment of culturally and linguistically rich lesson themes and grammatical concepts provides an excellent base for the textbook's engaging format and reading passages.

The outline of learning objectives is followed by a list of new vocabulary items ("New vocabulary corner") that are to be targeted through the reading passages. Vocabulary items are reviewed using drills and activities, with additional important vocabulary included at the end of the chapter. Primary vocabulary items are then recycled in the main lesson reading passages. Reading passages are accompanied by writing exercises, which are designed to elicit paragraph-length or longer written output through appealing prompts. It is useful that the reading passages can also be accessed via recordings on the accompanying DVD (recent printings of the book include the DVD material on a companion website—ed.), which may help to increase comprehension. Reading passages are described as "expository prose" (xxii) and continue to follow the series' two main characters, Michael Brown and Adnan Martini. Cultural content is provided throughout the book and through the reading passages, which are written from the point of view of Michael Brown, a nonnative learner of Arabic. This is a positive development for Arabic foreign-language textbooks, as some (see MacDonald, Badger, and Dasli 2006) criticize the notion of learning materials as overly focused on *correspondence* of reality in given communities of language use rather than *genesis* of reality on the part of the learners and their own local communities of practice. Another positive aspect of this textbook's reading passages is the inclusion of brief multipage texts that are both modified and authentic. While the authors acknowledge the debate surrounding the role of authenticity in foreign-language materials design, it remains unclear whether modified texts provide superior linguistic input (Mishan 2005, 24), something that should be examined via empirical evidence on learner comprehension of modified versus authentic texts. As these texts may provide less of a challenge for learners hoping to make the jump from novice to intermediate proficiency, the engaging topics within these reading passages may provide an excellent supplement to other textbook series with authentic, unmodified texts.

While providing an excellent intermediate-level textbook through engaging content and format, it should be noted that this series is designed for MSA-only instruction. As a recent study has shown knowledge of an Arabic spoken variety to be a better predictor of listening comprehension than knowledge of MSA (Trentman 2011), the textbook could be improved by providing a spoken-Arabic supplement. Even as results of the study by Emma Trentman (2011) may be affected by confounding factors not accounted for by the researcher (Alhawary 2018), inclusion of dialect-specific vocabulary provides an option for program directors desiring a pedagogical program and textbook that includes a dialect component. Still, for those desirous of MSA-only instruction, the second edition of *Ahlan wa Sahlan* for intermediate learners provides an excellent option, with content and topics worthy of praise.

References

Alhawary, Mohammad T. 2018. "Empirical Directions in the Future of Arabic Second Language Acquisition and Second Language Pedagogy." In *Handbook for Arabic Language Teaching Professionals in the 21st Century*, Vol. 2, ed. Kassem M. Wahba, Liz England, and Zeinab A. Taha, 408–21. New York: Routledge.

Azaz, Mahmoud. 2016. "Integrating the Genre-Based Approach into Teaching Writing in Arabic as a Foreign Language." *Journal of the Less Commonly Taught Languages* 19: 31–60.

Byrnes, Heidi, Cori Crane, Hiram H. Maxim, and Katherine A. Sprang. 2006. "Taking Text to Task: Issues and Choices in Curriculum Construction." *ITL: International Journal of Applied Linguistics* 152: 85–109.

Hyland, Ken. 2007. "Genre Pedagogy: Language, Literacy and L2 Writing Instruction." *Journal of Second Language Writing* 16, no. 3: 148–64.

MacDonald, Malcolm N., Richard Badger, and Maria Dasli. 2006. "Authenticity, Culture and Language Learning." *Language and Intercultural Communication* 6, no. 3–4: 250–61.

Mishan, Freda. 2005. *Designing Authenticity into Language Learning Materials*. Bristol, UK: Intellect.

Swender, Elvira, Daniel Conrad, and Robert Vicars. 2012. *ACTFL Proficiency Guidelines 2012*. Alexandria, VA: American Council for the Teaching of Foreign Languages.

Trentman, Emma. 2011. "L2 Arabic Dialect Comprehension: Empirical Evidence for the Transfer of Familiar Dialect Knowledge to Unfamiliar Dialects." *L2 Journal* 3, no. 1: 22–49.

REVIEW

Arabic Language in the Emirati Films: Linguistic and Cultural Window on Emirati Films

Nasser M. Isleem and Hajer Al Madhi.

San Bernardino, CA: CreateSpace Independent Publishing Platform, 2016. ix + 111 pp.

Reviewed by Maher Bahloul, American University of Sharjah

With *Arabic Language in the Emirati Films,* Nasser Isleem and Hajer Al Madhi join the growing field of edutainment and extend the life of a number of local cinematographic productions. Recent interest in language learning through film has attracted a number of researchers such as John Golden (2001), Nikos Theodosakis (2009), Maher Bahloul and Carolyn Graham (2012), Bahloul and Wafa Mezghani (2012), and Pierangela Diadori (2012), but works relevant for Arabic language learning are scarce.

While traditional language textbooks rely on a selection of texts, passages, or conversations written to suit the desired level or taken from authentic materials, the authors here adopt a completely different approach, using five Emirati films as the unique source of language learning. The book is a welcome addition, but its overall content and structure would benefit from greater elaboration, clarification, and consistency.

The book is divided into a five-page introduction and five chapters of eighteen to twenty-four pages. The book is written per the American ACTFL guidelines to suit intermediate Arabic learners. Each chapter includes four sections: reading and comprehension, vocabulary and expressions, conversation and dialogue, and writing. The authors claim that the book provides access to language, culture, and film.

They also suggest that the book may be used as a primary textbook or a reader at the intermediate level.

Each chapter relates to one Emirati-produced film and focuses on current changes and dynamics within Emirati society. The films are *Sea Shadow* by Nawaf Al-Janahi (2011), *Sun Dress* by Saeed Salmeen Al-Murry (2014), *Grandmother's Farm* by Ahmed Zain (2013), *City of Life* by Ali Mustafa (2010), and *Bint Mariam* by Saeed Salmeen Al-Murry (2009).

Chapter 1 deals with relationships between men and women, and parents and children, and treats issues such as love, hate, deception, harassment, and life's ups and downs. Through the life stories of two young Emirati men, chapter 2 shows the gap between modern life and traditional life. It also shows significant social class differences within Emirati society through relationships between Emirati men and foreign young ladies, a complex issue within Emirati society. Other social issues involving expatriates are also addressed. Chapter 3 relates to one of the major passions of Emiratis, desert life, and entertainment. The film deals with a supposedly relaxing trip to a desert farm that turns into a dreadful nightmare. Chapter 4 focuses on social marginalization through the story of a forbidden love between a young man and a hearing-impaired young woman. The last chapter deals with the issue of early marriage and shows the extent to which women lack basic rights and how culture and beliefs tend to justify such practices. All in all, the content is quite varied and exposes learners to highly functional daily language.

Language is introduced through utterance lists in each chapter, ranging from 59 to 107 utterances of one to seven words in length. All utterances are in Emirati Arabic, a Gulf dialect distinct from Levantine, Egyptian, and North African dialects.

Each chapter starts with a two-page introduction, including a film synopsis and general questions, which act as a general introduction to the film's major events and key characters. Four sections follow, containing a large number of tasks, exercises, and assignments. While the number of tasks varies by chapter, the focus in each section is similar. Some tasks are meant to be done in class, while others are to be completed as homework assignments. Most importantly, all tasks are designed to promote language learning through interaction and oral communication.

The first section of each chapter, titled "Reading and Comprehension," includes two exercises, one related to the film's story, whereabouts, themes, and learners' opinions, and the other involving internet-based assignments to be presented in class. It is unclear why this section is titled as it is since there are no reading assignments nor comprehension tasks. The second section, "Words and Expressions," includes selected utterances from the films with meanings given in Standard Arabic and English. Learners are expected to familiarize themselves with these expressions as they watch the film. Most important are the various exercises within this section that are meant to boost learners' understanding of the words and expressions. This is the longest section of each chapter, demonstrating the salience of vocabulary learning as a key to language learning. The third section, "Speaking and Discussing," includes five to seven exercises all designed to promote oral production by addressing the films' themes and characters or acting out roles of particular film characters. In addition, some exercises focus on intercultural communication and awareness of local cultural dynamics. The fourth section is very brief, including two to four written assignments relevant to the films: some of these assignments include short, straightforward tasks, while others are complex with several writing tasks. Given the nature of the issues related to Emirati culture, it is clear that learners will have to do more research to be able to understand and reflect upon those issues.

Overall, the book is quite successful in presenting innovative content and promoting the use of film in learning Arabic. It also provides an incentive for cinematic production, as films may become important classroom instructional materials. However, a number of items call for revision.

There are a number of issues related to language use in this book. First, the book's cover gives the impression that this is a bilingual book: in fact, it is an entirely monolingual Arabic book. All introductions, explanations, instructions, exercises, and assignments are in Arabic. It is worth mentioning, however, that the "Words and Expressions" sections include English translations, and there is at least one Arabic-to-English exercise in each chapter. Thus, the book may not be of great value for learners of Arabic with no advanced proficiency. Second, there is a mixture of Standard Arabic and Emirati dialect within exercises and assignments, while the films are fully in Emirati Arabic. If the objective is to promote the local language, it is probably more beneficial to make use of Emirati Arabic throughout, making the book an effective resource for learning Emirati Arabic without including Standard Arabic. Third, the written forms of Arabic utterances do not provide systematic and adequate access to their pronunciation in Emirati Arabic. If the authors provided the phonetic transcription of vocabulary items, it would be easier for learners to practice them. Short of that, learners have to rely on recording the utterances from the film itself to be able to access the adequate pronunciation. While this is what the authors had in mind, it is not an easy and practical task. Finally, it is unclear why the authors isolate a couple of Emirati sounds—namely, the affricate /t͡ʃ/ and the approximant /j/—as they replace the Standard Arabic /k/ and /ʒ/, respectively. They systematically present these in parentheses as if they were exceptions or some sort of abnormality. There is really no need to treat such sounds differently from other sounds when Emirati Arabic shows phonetic and phonological differences from Standard Arabic.

There are a number of inconsistencies in the book. First, the initial two pages of each chapter include three assignments that play an introductory role for a chapter's content. These should have been included in an introduction for the sake of consistency. Second, the book mixes the use of Arabic and Indian numerals. It is unclear whether this mixing is done intentionally, but consistency is desirable. Third, while each chapter includes four sections, the gap between their quantities is pronounced. The second and third sections in each chapter represent more than 90 percent of the chapters' content. A better balance could have been achieved if the authors had limited the major chapter sections to two instead of four. Finally, the order of the films appearing on the introductory table (p. vi) should have mirrored the order of the book's chapters.

The book would benefit from the addition of film scripts in an appendix, and from an index. With a script, learners could, for instance, locate utterances within their respective contexts. They would also have easy access to other utterances in the film that have not been included in the vocabulary section. Moreover, students could select passages from the script and act them out after they watch the film. In addition to the script, the book could have included an appendix with maps and pictures related to the films' events. Films are visually rich resources, and including a selection of visuals would make the chapters more appealing, as some assignments could draw on such visuals. Finally, an index of names, places, cultural events, and festivities would constitute a welcome addition to the textbook, allowing learners to extend their knowledge of Emirati linguistic and cultural landscapes.

Some other observations are in order. First, the authors claim that their choice of films has taken into consideration students' tastes, academic levels, and language proficiency. It remains unclear how such a claim may be justified since no survey results have been presented. Second, the films are not part of the book; that is, although the authors mention that the films are available in university libraries and may be purchased through film stores and relevant websites, finding them may not be that simple. Had the authors provided a DVD or protected links, access to the films would be facilitated. Third, the book is designed for students who are proficient in Standard and Emirati Arabic. As such, learners of either language will not be able to use the book. This is an unfortunate limitation.

The authors stress the importance of film in Arabic learning, given its power to motivate learners and expose them to local language and culture. The various themes of the films expose learners to a variety of language use in a number of different cultural settings. The book is thus a desirable addition to the current Arabic textbooks that focus on day-to-day oral communicative functions. However, much improvement is needed in both the book's form and content, as highlighted in this review.

References

Bahloul, Maher, and Carolyn Graham. 2012. *Lights! Camera! Action and the Brain: The Use of Film in Education.* London: Cambridge Scholars.

Bahloul, Maher, and Wafa Mezghani. 2012. "From an Expatriate Diary: Learning through Film-making." In *Lights! Camera! Action and the Brain: The Use of Film in Education,* ed. Maher Bahloul and Carolyn Graham, 218–39. London: Cambridge Scholars.

Diadori, Pierangela. 2012. "Foreign Language Learning through Filmmaking." In *Lights! Camera! Action and the Brain: The Use of Film in Education,* ed. Maher Bahloul and Carolyn Graham, 258–80. London: Cambridge Scholars.

Golden, John. 2001. *Reading in the Dark: Using Film as a Tool in the English Classroom.* Urbana, IL: National Council of Teachers of English.

Theodosakis, Nikos. 2009. *The Director in the Classroom: How Filmmaking Inspires Learning.* San Diego, CA: Tech4Learning.

REVIEW

Advanced Arabic Literary Reader: For Students of Modern Standard Arabic

Jonas M. Elbousty and Muhammad Ali Aziz.

London: Routledge, 2016. xiv + 390 pp. ISBN: 9781138828698. Paperback, $65.95.

Reviewed by Sawad Hussain, Translator and literary critic

Described as a collection of literary extracts from across the Arab world that take into consideration each country and gender as well as prominent and emerging voices, the *Advanced Arabic Literary Reader* is written entirely in Modern Standard Arabic. It is meant to be suitable for both classroom and independent study environments, serving as an introduction to the rich world of modern Arabic literature. The stated objective in the preface is to develop the skills necessary for reading comprehension of authentic literary texts from the Arab world.

The *Reader* consists of sixty excerpts from novels and short stories. There are nineteen countries represented in all; the editors confess to omitting Somalia and Comoros because of the "scarcity of Arabic literary narratives." The sheer geographical diversity of the chosen texts must be applauded. There are the conventional nations whose narratives are embedded in the mainstream consciousness: Egypt, Lebanon, Morocco, Sudan, and Syria. Then there are unsung modern works from less-celebrated countries in today's literary arena: Yemen, Oman, Bahrain, Qatar, Kuwait, Libya, and Mauritania. Given that most, if not all, current literary readers on the market primarily focus on literature from the first list of countries, this carefully curated compendium of texts from underrepresented countries is crucial in aiding students to understand the true diversity of the Arab world.

The *Reader* is wanting, however, once the equality of genders is considered—a mere eleven of the sixty texts are penned by women. Undeniably, an effort has been made to include female authors, with iconic figures such as Ahlam Mosteghanemi, Nawal El Saadawi, and Hanan al-Shaykh featured. But one is left wondering where the other female luminaries of Arabic literature, such as Sahar Khalifa (Palestine), Alia Mamdouh (Iraq), Hoda Barakat (Lebanon), and Radwa Ashour (Egypt), are; these are novelists who are found in the *Encyclopedia of Arabic Literature* and who by no means are new to the literary scene. Such emerging female voices as Maha Hassan (Syria) and Reneé Hayek (Lebanon)—thrice-longlisted for the International Prize for Arabic Fiction—and bestselling writer Bouthāyna Al-Īssa (Kuwait) also fail to make it into the collection. There is no shortage of female literary greats as well as more recently established writers to choose from. As such, the *Reader* has failed somewhat in providing an accurate representation of the modern Arabic literary tradition, which is an aspect that the editors should consider addressing in future editions.

The structure of each chapter is as follows: (a) biography of the author, (b) prereading activity, (c) summary of the excerpted novel or short story as a whole, (d) excerpt, (e) comprehension exercise, (f) sentence-matching exercise, (g) fill-in-the-blanks exercise, (h) true/false statement exercise, (i) discussion prompts, (j) translation section, and (k) writing prompts.

The texts are not organized in any sort of chronological or alphabetical order. Before delving into the exercises and how they combine to provide excellent scaffolding for the student in further understanding the text at hand, I must draw attention to the availability of audio recordings for each of the sixty texts. The audio files are generously free on the Routledge website, and those educators wanting to ensure that the grammatical aspects of the language are not forgotten in the flurry of content interpretation will be happy to know that the texts are read aloud with *i'rāb*. These can be used as a review to get students to vowel a few lines before listening to the audio.

Each chapter provides the most comprehensive approach to a literary text that I have come across for Arabic language learners, encouraging them to engage with the text on a range of levels, using different skills in the process. The biography section is limited to an author's origin, education, and key works. The prereading section is made up of two questions: the first always asks students to do further research on the author and write a paragraph or present their findings; the second question is linked to a theme explored in the author's work. For example, for Hanan al-Shaykh, students are meant to comment on patriarchy in the West versus the East, and for Tayeb Salih the question is about the effects of Western society on Arab customs.

The summary (generally 170 words each) of the novel or short story helps contextualize and situate the excerpt. But more importantly, the summaries repeatedly use key words in Arabic that teachers would want their students to use when describing a literary work. With ease, these summaries give students the lexicon and structure to use when they need to write an impactful summary rather than a list-like series of events. The editors have also wisely left out the conclusion in the summaries, in case the student is spurred to continue reading a work outside of the textbook. There is a summary for every text, with the exception of Hanan al-Shaykh's *Man Yuʿallimunī al-Biyānū*, which appears to be a simple oversight.

The ensuing comprehension section consists of five questions, ranging from those more explicit in nature to more inferential ones. The next exercise of matching statements is based on events in the excerpt. The fill-in-the-blanks section is well written for each chapter, with a different part of speech tested in each question. The true/false statement section heralds a shift from straightforward event identification and pushes the student further. What would make each of these five carefully crafted exercises—from the comprehension questions to the true/false sections—even more beneficial would be an answer key at the back of the book or available separately online. An answer key would help individual learners or those simply wanting to check their work to see if they have truly understood.

The discussion questions encourage students to speak about more complex ideas such as "Explain what character X means when they say Y" and "How do you imagine the end of this novel?"

The Arabic–English translation section is on average one hundred words, with the translation text being an extract from the excerpt itself. However, once again, there should be at least one example of how this could be translated into English in an answer key so that independent students can see if they are missing an implied past tense, if their word order needs to be rearranged when moving between Arabic and English, or how they can keep true to the rhythm of the writing.

The final exercise consists of two writing prompts, each suggesting a 150–200-word answer. This section ties in very well with each of the texts explored as the prompts successfully tease out themes for students to further debate. For example, the prompts for Saud Al-Sanousi's *Sāq al-Bambū* are "How does one keep family together in the face of societal pressure and economic strife?" and "How does death affect us?"

Although there is a disappointing lack of female authors properly represented in this Arabic literary reader, from a pedagogical perspective, it is a force to be reckoned with. There is no other resource in the field at the moment that successfully takes students on the journey of delving into such a breadth of texts while using all four skills and pushing them to think outside their usual boundaries of what is Arabic literature.

Contributors

Maher Bahloul is an associate professor at the American University of Sharjah. His areas of research and teaching include theoretical and applied linguistics, sociolinguistics, and teaching and learning through the arts. He is the author of *Structure and Function of the Arabic Verb* (Routledge, 2008) and numerous articles on Arabic language and linguistics.

John Eisele is an associate professor at the College of William and Mary. His research has focused on a wide variety of topics dealing with Arabic language, linguistics, and culture, including tense and aspect, word play, sound symbolism, and the Hollywood "Eastern" genre. From 1999 to 2007 he was the executive director of the American Association of Teachers of Arabic and is a past recipient of Fulbright and National Endowment for the Humanities fellowships. He is currently working with Driss Cherkaoui to produce a new curriculum and textbook series for Arabic, both formal and dialectal, with support from the Department of Education.

Shehdeh Fareh is professor of linguistics at the University of Sharjah, where he is currently the director of the Language Institute. He has published many articles, translated several books into Arabic and English, and is the principal author of a series of English foreign-language books. His research interests include contrastive discourse analysis, teaching English as a foreign language, and translation.

Peter Glanville is an assistant professor of Arabic at the University of Maryland, College Park, where he is also director of the Arabic Flagship Program. He holds a PhD in Arabic Studies from the University of Texas at Austin, and an MS in Applied Linguistics from the University of Edinburgh. His research interests center on Arabic language pedagogy and on Arabic derivational morphology. He is the author of *The Lexical Semantics of the Arabic Verb* (Oxford University Press, 2018), which examines the relationship between linguistic form and meaning as it pertains to the verb patterns of Arabic.

Uri Horesh is a British Academy Postdoctoral Fellow in the Department of Language and Linguistics at the University of Essex. His research focuses on Levantine dialects of Arabic (mostly Palestinian and Jordanian) as well as Modern Hebrew from a variationist sociolinguistic perspective. He has published, inter alia, in *Journal of Sociolinguistics, Language and Linguistics Compass, Journal of Jewish Languages, Zeitschrift für arabische Linguistik,* and *The Encyclopedia of Arabic Language and Linguistics.*

Sawad Hussain holds an MA in Modern Arabic Literature from the School of Oriental and African Studies. She was co-revising editor of the Arabic–English side of the 2014 *Oxford Arabic Dictionary.* She regularly translates and critiques Arabic literature. Her latest translation is of a Jordanian speculative-fiction novel by Fadi Zaghmout, and she is currently translating a Kuwaiti historical-fiction novel by Saud al-Sanousi, to appear in 2019.

Yahya Kharrat is an assistant professor of Arabic at Western University in London, Ontario, Canada, and holds a PhD in applied linguistics from the University of Kansas. His areas of interest include Arabic dialects, applied linguistics, and pedagogy of Arabic as a second language.

Thomas A. Leddy-Cecere is a faculty member in sociolinguistics at Bennington College. His research interests comprise language variation and change in both synchronic and diachronic applications, and his current projects include the study of contact-induced grammatical change in the history of Arabic and the sociolinguistic analysis of dialect accommodation phenomena among transnational Arabic-speaking populations.

Janelle Moser is a PhD candidate in the Graduate Interdisciplinary Second Language Acquisition and Teaching Program at the University of Arizona. Her research interests include vocabulary teaching and learning, materials evaluation and design, the corpus-based approach to foreign language teaching and learning, and language-program administration. Her forthcoming dissertation focuses on Arabic as a foreign language commercial materials evaluation and design from a variety of popular second-language acquisition theories and perspectives.

Paul A. Sundberg is director of the Gulf Arabic Program in Al Buraimi, Sultanate of Oman. He holds an MS in Linguistics from Georgetown University, an MA in Arabic Studies from the American University in Cairo, and a PhD in Educational Psychology from the University of Illinois at Urbana-Champaign. He was born in Saudi Arabia and began Arabic study in first grade in a (Saudi) Aramco school. He has lived a total of twenty-eight years in the Middle East, including Egypt, Jordan, and Kuwait.

Maria L. Swanson is an assistant professor at the U.S. Naval Academy. She graduated from Moscow State University, majoring in Arabic philology and history, and she holds a PhD in Middle Eastern Studies from the University of Arizona. She has been teaching Arabic and Russian as foreign languages in the United States and in Europe and has spent eight years in the Arabic world working as a translator. Her research interests include Arabic–Russian cultural ties, Mahjari literature, some sociolinguistics aspects of Arabic language, and second language pedagogy.

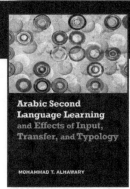

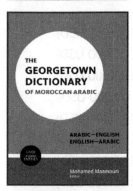

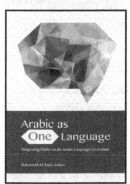

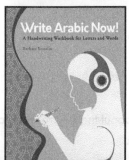

Al-'Arabiyya Submission Guidelines

Al-'Arabiyya welcomes scholarly and pedagogical articles and book reviews that contribute to the advancement of study, criticism, research, and teaching in the fields of Arabic language, linguistics, and literature. We also consider responses and comments on articles published in previous issues. Review articles are also welcome; contact the editor to propose one.

Please address all correspondence regarding submissions to the Editor, *Al-'Arabiyya* Journal, aataeditor@aataweb.org.

General Guidelines

Authors are encouraged to present an original, scholarly contribution or a perceptive restructuring of existing knowledge. *All articles are subject to a peer review process. Previously published pieces or those being considered for publication elsewhere will not be accepted.*

Book reviews are commissioned by the book review editor. Reviews of current and recently published textbooks are particularly welcome. Please propose a book review to the book review editor prior to submission at aatabookrevieweditor@aataweb.org.

Submission Procedures

Submissions are accepted by email attachment only. Please attach both a PDF version and an original Word document, including an abstract in English of 100–150 words. To aid the blind review process, remove author's name and identifying information from the article and include a cover sheet with author's name, mailing address, email address, telephone number, academic affiliation, and title of the article.

Article length: 8,000 words max (Times New Roman, 12 pt.). Review article length: 1,500–2,000 words max. Book review length: 750–1,250 words max. Doulos SIL fonts must be used for transliterated text/words. SIL's Scheherazade font must be used for Arabic terms. Reviews must be in English. Reviews previously appearing in print or online will not be accepted. Articles in Arabic must use SIL's Scheherazade font.

Submission must conform to *Al-'Arabiyya* style and writing guidelines. These are posted online on *Al-'Arabiyya* website: http://www.aataweb.org/alarabiyya.